LIFE AFTER DEBT

How to Repair Your Credit and Get Out of Debt Once and For All

by Bob Hammond

LIFE
AFTER
DEBT

How to Repair Your Credit and Get Out of Debt Once and For All

by Bob Hammond

CAREER PRESS
180 Fifth Avenue
P.O. Box 34
Hawthorne, NJ 07507
1-800-CAREER-1
201-427-0229 (outside U.S.)
FAX: 201-427-2037

LIFE AFTER DEBT
HOW TO REPAIR YOUR CREDIT AND GET OUT OF DEBT ONCE AND FOR ALL
ISBN 1-56414-101-2, $14.95
Cover design by A Good Thing, Inc.
Printed in the U.S.A. by Book-mart Press

To order this title by mail, please include price as noted above, $2.50 handling per order, and $1.00 for each book ordered. Send to: Career Press, Inc., 180 Fifth Ave., P.O. Box 34, Hawthorne, NJ 07507

Or call toll-free 1-800-CAREER-1 (Canada: 201-427-0229) to order using VISA or MasterCard, or for further information on books from Career Press.

Library of Congress Cataloging-in-Publication Data

Hammond, Bob.
    Life after debt : how to repair your credit and get out of debt once and for all / by Bob Hammond.
       p. cm.
    Includes index.
    ISBN 1-56414-101-2 : $14.95
    1. Consumer credit--United States. 2. Debtor and creditor--United States. I. Title.
    HG3756.U54H365 1993
    332.7'43--dc20   93-22389
                                      CIP

WARNING

THIS BOOK CONTAINS CERTAIN confidential information that could easily be subject to abuse or misuse. Neither the author nor the publisher encourages, endorses, or recommends the use of any of these methods as a means to defraud or violate the rights of any individual or organization. The reader is therefore encouraged to use this material responsibly.

The author is not engaged in rendering any legal service. The services of a professional are recommended if legal advice or assistance is needed. The author and publisher disclaim any responsibility for personal loss or liabilities caused by the use or misuse of any information presented herein.

CONTENTS

FOREWORD

As HEAD OF A LARGE NETWORK of independent credit consultants, I am often asked to recommend books for consumers and professionals.

Bob Hammond's latest book, *Life after Debt*, breaks new ground. It is by far the most comprehensive book on consumer credit available anywhere. I found it thoroughly entertaining, informative, and easy to read.

Other books may be limited to such specific topics as billing-error disputes or bankruptcy, are poorly written, or seem to be addressed to individuals with backgrounds in high finance. *Life after Debt* is not only well written, it's easy for the average person to follow and understand. It provides consumers with realistic, practical solutions for their debt and credit problems. It avoids the scams and unworkable techniques found in so-called "credit repair" manuals and provides its readers with proven methods that work.

Life after Debt is destined to set a trend in helping people understand the credit system. Therefore, *Life after Debt* receives my highest approval and recommendation and should be made required reading for every consumer.

Leonard B. Robin, Chief Executive Officer
Fresh Start Financial Services

FOREWORD

PREFACE

Upon graduation from high school, Abel received his first credit card from his parents. He applied for a student loan and headed off to college.

He graduated with a master's degree in psychology, and within three years he was earning $40,000 a year as a counselor in a private treatment center. Then there was a funding problem, and he was out of work and $84,000 in debt.

Abel borrowed money from his parents and collected unemployment benefits. For six months, he was able to maintain his standard of living by using his credit cards to obtain cash advances. Then the money stopped coming. His lines of credit were all overextended.

After his unemployment benefits ran out, Abel fell into a deep state of depression. His car was in need of major repairs and was about to be repossessed. Creditors threatened legal action. Bankruptcy appeared to be the only way out.

If only Abel had known the secrets of *Life after Debt.*

Most books on consumer credit tell people what they already know—"Pay your bills!" But what about the person who just can't pay anything right now?

Life after Debt makes a dramatic departure from traditional approaches to personal finance. Not a rehash of old information, it attacks the root causes of indebtedness and teaches people how to solve their credit problems—once and for all.

My previous books, *Credit Secrets: How to Erase Bad Credit* and *How to Beat the Credit Bureaus: The Insider's Guide to Consumer Credit* (Paladin Press), give readers a revealing, if not controversial, overview of the credit system. Both books provide unique insights into the operations of the major credit-reporting agencies and teach consumers how to remove negative information from their files.

Life after Debt takes you a few steps further. It teaches you to deal effectively with every aspect of the credit system and offers workable solutions for every kind of financial difficulty. It provides easy-to-follow instructions for reducing debts, raising credit limits, and increasing cash flow.

Other books on consumer credit often view bankruptcy as a consumer's only real alternative to overwhelming debt problems. Most individuals, however, require more than just a Band-Aid solution to their problems.

Life after Debt will teach you how to get out of debt without bankruptcy or borrowing. Or, if you decide that bankruptcy is the best option for you, it shows you how to reestablish excellent credit in less than thirty days. Written to meet the needs of people in every situation— regardless of income—this book includes special sections devoted to the needs of women, minorities, divorced people, and military families.

Destined to be controversial, it reveals inside information not previously available to the general public. For example, file segregation—the only 100-percent effective method of "erasing" all negative credit records overnight— is so powerful that certain consultants charge their clients more than $1,000 for five minutes' work. And yes, it's completely legal.

Life after Debt also teaches readers how to create an "instant" credit history dating back up to ten years. This recently discovered technique was developed by a special consultant to undercover agents in Southern California.

Endorsed by nationally known consumer advocates, attorneys, and business professionals, *Life after Debt* is the most comprehensive guide of its kind. Not just a program of positive thinking, it is a program of positive action, providing easy-to-follow steps to solvency and success.

Dedicated to the millions of Americans who are hurting financially right now, *Life after Debt* offers realistic hope and healing. I hope you find it entertaining, enlightening, and educational. Most of all, I pray that it will empower you to become free—once and for all—from the tyranny of financial bondage.

INTRODUCTION

*Why Read This
Guide?*

A FEW INTERESTING STATISTICS
ABOUT DEBT IN AMERICA

• Fifty-nine million Americans are *addicted* to shopping
or spending.

• About 1 million Americans filed for personal bankruptcy in
1991. That's nearly one in every 200 people.

• The number of nonbusiness bankruptcy filings rose to
580,459 for the year ending 30 June 1989. That figure was
up 10 percent from the same period the previous year,
according to the administrative office of the U.S. Courts.

• Individual consumers incur approximately $2 to $3 billion
a month in consumer debt. Collectively, we owe $3 trillion.

• Over 200 million credit cards are in circulation, up
from 120 million in 1980. The average balance per card is
$1,300, compared to $500 just a decade ago.

• The number of people behind on car payments has risen
25 percent in the past few years.

• Nearly 5 percent of homeowners are behind on their
mortgage payments.

• More than 70 percent of adult American consumers

have at least one derogatory remark on their credit reports.

• Nearly 46 percent of all credit reports contain inaccurate, obsolete, or misleading information.

• The Federal Trade Commission (FTC) receives more complaints related to credit-reporting abuses than all other matters combined.

• More than 40 million American adults do not qualify for a major credit card.

• One out of three people who actually get a look at their files seek changes, and 75 percent are entitled to them.

• A recent study of 6,000 credit reports revealed a 47-percent error factor in reporting information.

TEN WARNING SIGNALS TO TELL IF YOU ARE IN TROUBLE

Listed below are ten warning signals that can help you determine whether *you* are headed for financial trouble. If any of these conditions apply to you, it's time to take a closer look at your budget. If three or more apply, you are in financial difficulty and should seek assistance as soon as possible.

1. Using credit to buy things you used to be able to buy with cash
2. Getting new loans or extensions to pay your debts
3. Paying only the minimum amount due on charge cards
4. Receiving overdue notices from creditors
5. Using savings to pay bills that you used to pay from checking
6. Borrowing on life insurance with little chance of repayment
7. Depending on overtime pay to make ends meet each month

8. Using your checking account "overdraft" to pay regular bills

9. Juggling rent or mortgage money to pay other debts

10. Using credit card cash advances to help pay living expenses

• • • • •

More people filed personal bankruptcy in America last year than graduated from college.

Until now, people with credit problems could only go to books that offered tedious budget plans or vague interpretations of federal consumer law. These books often assume the reader's ability to adhere to strict payment schedules or implement complex legal strategies. They fail, however, to address the real problem: *most of us are not lawyers or accountants*.

Few of us are inclined to carry out technical legal maneuvers or sophisticated financial strategies. Even fewer people can afford the services of a good financial advisor. Sometimes people just aren't able to pay anything to anyone. Millions of Americans are living on the edge of financial disaster, surviving only on the hope of next week's paycheck.

Life after Debt is a primer, the first of its kind, which teaches people to play the credit game—and win—regardless of their starting point. It provides practical solutions for every kind of credit problem through case histories, sample letters, and easy-to-follow procedures.

The purpose of this book is to help you break the bondage of debt and start over. It will guide you from the ravaging tyranny of financial slavery to the light of freedom. You will come to know the insidious nature of the beast as you discover how its ensnaring web weaves its way into your life. You

will learn to fight back against and unfair system—and win
—for yourself and your family.

May the eyes of your understanding be enlightened.

PART ONE

Is There Really Life after Debt?

CHAPTER 1

Counting the Cost of Credit

RON AND ANGELA DECIDED TO CELEBRATE *their first anniversary together by purchasing a top-of-the-line stereo system. Still living on a shoestring, they wanted to be sure of getting top value for their money, so they spent weeks reading stereo magazines and catalogs, visiting showrooms, and getting advice from their friends. Finally, they settled on the components they wanted. Then they went to the dealer they had chosen and, after a couple of hours of bargaining, agreed on a total price that was considerably under the list prices displayed on the floor. They signed an installment contract offered by the store and raced home with their car full of stereo components, feeling like robbers who had made a daring getaway.*

What's wrong with this picture?

The total interest Ron and Angela were committed to paying far exceeded the total dollar amount they had saved by their careful bargaining. It had never occurred to either Ron or Angela that they could profit by putting as much effort into shopping for credit as they had into choosing their stereo components.

7

Credit issuers are smart. They know human nature and buying habits inside out. That's why they're getting richer while you're getting deeper into debt. They have joined forces with the advertising industry to convince you that you can have everything your heart desires right now. Even things you didn't know you wanted.

Consumers are made to feel guilty for not using credit or for not having a credit card. Have you ever made a purchase and been asked, "Will that be on your account today?" What the clerk is really saying is, "You are worthy enough to have a credit card, aren't you?"

People are fooled into becoming debtors by thinking of debt as credit. Some people even get a certain amount of gratification from flashing a wallet full of plastic in front of others as if it were some type of status symbol. How many times have you engaged in this game of credit card one-upmanship to see who can display the most prestigious credit card?

For most people, debt (credit) represents a fair exchange for the life-style they enjoy. Others find it a consuming whirlpool that sucks their creative talents continuously. These people have become unemployed or have lost their economic base. For them, debt is no longer a slight inconvenience—it is a rapidly growing monster. They experience a special type of hell with every mail delivery containing bills and registered letters. The stories they have heard concerning bill collectors, repossessions, and foreclosures take on a frightening reality. These people assume a sense of desperation, which is instantly communicated to potential employers or sources of income. These people may as well have a flashing neon sign on their foreheads . . . *loser*. This sets up a vicious cycle. Debts cause desperation, desperation turns off employers, and debts get bigger.

The cycle begins when you promise to pay in the future

for something you receive in the present. It starts when you charge a meal on your credit card, pay for an appliance on the installment plan, or take out a loan to pay for a house, schooling, or vacations. With credit, you can enjoy your purchase while you're paying for it—or you can make a purchase when you're lacking ready cash.

But there are strings attached. There's no such thing as a free lunch. And what is borrowed must be paid back.

If you are thinking of borrowing or opening a credit account, your first step should be to figure out how much it will cost you and whether you can afford it.

FINANCE CHARGES AND ANNUAL PERCENTAGE RATE

Credit costs vary. By remembering two terms, you can compare credit prices from different sources. Under truth-in-lending laws, the creditor must tell you—in writing and before you sign any agreement—the finance charge and the annual percentage rate (APR).

The *finance charge* is the total dollar amount you pay to use credit. It includes interest fees, as well as service charges and some credit-related insurance premiums. For example, borrowing $100 for a year might cost you $10 in interest. If there was also a service charge of $1, the finance charge would be $11.

The *annual percentage rate* is the percentage cost (or relative cost) of credit on a yearly basis. This is your key to comparing costs, regardless of the amount of credit or how long you have to repay it.

Again, suppose you borrow $100 for one year and pay a finance charge of $10. If you can keep the entire $100 for the whole year and then pay back $110 at the end of the year, you are paying an APR of 10 percent. But, if you repay the

$100 and finance charge (a total of $110) in twelve monthly installments, you don't really get to use $100 for the whole year. In fact, you get to use less and less of that $100 each month. In this case, the $10 charge for credit amounts to an APR of 18 percent.

All creditors—banks, stores, car dealers, credit card companies, finance companies, etc.—must state the cost of their credit in terms of the finance charge and the APR. Federal law does not set interest rates or other credit charges. But it does require their disclosure so that you can compare credit costs. The law says there are two pieces of information that must be shown to you before you sign a credit contract or use a credit card—the finance charge and the APR.

COMPARISON

Even when you understand the terms a creditor is offering, it's easy to underestimate the difference in dollars various terms can make. Suppose you're buying a $7,500 car. You put $1,500 down and need to borrow $6,000. Compare the three credit arrangements shown in the chart at the top of page 11. How do these choices stack up? The answer depends partly on what you need.

The lowest cost loan is available from Creditor A at an APR of 14 percent over three years. If you were looking for lower monthly payments, you could get them by paying the loan off over a longer period of time. However, you would have to pay more in total costs.

A loan from Creditor B—also at a 14 percent APR but for four years—will add about $488 to your finance charge.

If that four-year loan were available only from Creditor C, the APR of 15 percent would add another $145 or so to your finance charges as compared with Creditor B.

Other factors—such as the size of the down payment—will also make a difference. Be sure to look at all the terms before you make your choice.

CREDITOR	APR	LENGTH OF LOAN	MONTHLY PAYMENT	TOTAL FINANCE	TOTAL
Charge payment A	14%	3 Years	$205.07	$1,383.52	$7,382
Charge payment B	14%	4 Years	$163.96	$1,870.08	$7,870
Charge payment C	15%	4 Years	$166.98	$2,015.04	$8,015

COST OF OPEN-END CREDIT

Open-end credit includes bank and department store credit cards, gasoline company cards, home equity lines, and check overdraft accounts that let you write checks for more than your actual balance with the bank. Open-end credit can be used again and again, generally until you reach a certain prearranged borrowing limit. Truth-in-lending laws require that open-end creditors tell you the terms of the credit plan so that you can shop and compare the costs involved.

When you're shopping for an open-end plan, the APR you're quoted represents only the periodic rate that you will be charged, figured on a yearly basis. (For instance, a creditor that charges 1 1/2 percent interest each month would quote you an APR of 18 percent.) Annual membership fees, transaction charges, and points are listed separately; they are not included in the APR. Keep this in mind and compare *all* the costs involved in the plans, not just the APR.

Creditors must tell you when the finance charges begin on your account, so you know how much time you have to pay your bill before a finance charge is added. Creditors may give you a twenty-five-day grace period, for example, to pay your balance in full before making you pay a finance charge.

Creditors also must tell you the method they use to figure

the balance on which you pay a finance charge; the interest rate they charge is applied to this balance to come up with the finance charge. Creditors use a number of different methods to arrive at the balance. Study them carefully; they can affect your finance charge significantly.

For instance, some creditors, take the amount you owed at the beginning of the billing cycle and subtract any payments you made during that cycle. Purchases are not counted. This is called the *adjusted balance* method.

Another is the *previous balance* method. Creditors simply use the amount owed at the beginning of the billing cycle to come up with the finance charge.

Under one of the most common methods, the *average daily balance* method, creditors add your balances for each day in the billing cycle and then divide that total by the number of days in the cycle. Payments made during the cycle are subtracted in arriving at the daily amounts, and, depending on the plan, new purchases may or may not be included.

Under another method, the *two-cycle average daily balance* method, creditors use the average daily balances for two billing-cycles to compute your finance charge. Again, payments will be taken into account in figuring the balances, but new purchases may or may not be included.

Be aware that the amount of the finance charge may vary considerably depending on the method used, even for the same pattern of purchases and payments.

If you receive a credit card offer or an application, the creditor must give you information about APR and other important terms of the plan at that time. Likewise, with a home-equity plan, information must be given to you with an application.

Truth-in-lending laws do not set the rates or tell the creditor how to calculate finance charges—they only require that the creditor tell you the method that it uses. You should ask for an explanation of terms you don't understand.

BILLING ERRORS

Month after month Janice was billed for a necklace she never ordered and never got. Finally, she tore up her bill and mailed back the pieces just to try to explain things to a person instead of a computer.

There's an easier, more effective way to straighten out these errors. The Fair Credit Billing Act requires creditors to correct errors promptly and without damage to your credit rating.

The law defines a billing error as any charge:

• for something you didn't buy or for a purchase made by someone not authorized to use your account
• that is not properly identified on your bill or is for an amount different from the actual purchase price or that was entered on a date different from the purchase date
• for something that you did not accept on delivery or that was not delivered according to agreement

Billing errors also include:

• mistakes in arithmetic
• failure to reflect a payment or other credit to your account
• failure to mail the statement to your current address, provided you notified the creditor of an address change at least twenty days before the end of the billing period
• a questionable item, or one for which you need additional information

If you think your bill is wrong or want more information about it, follow these steps:

13

1. Notify the creditor in writing within sixty days after the bill was mailed. Be sure to write to the address the creditor lists for billing inquiries and to tell the creditor:

A. your name and account number

B. that you believe the bill contains an error and why you believe it is wrong

C. the date and amount of the suspected error or the item you want explained

2. Pay all parts of the bill that are not in dispute. While waiting for an answer, you do not have to pay the amount in question (the "disputed amount") or any minimum payments or finance charges that apply to it.

The creditor must acknowledge your letter within thirty days, unless the problem can be resolved within that time. Within two billing periods, but in no case longer than ninety days, either your account must be corrected or you must be told why the creditor believes the bill is correct.

If the creditor made a mistake, you do not have to pay any finance charges on the disputed amount. Your account must be corrected, and you must be sent an explanation of any amount you still owe.

If no error is found, the creditor must send you an explanation of the reasons for that determination and promptly send a statement of what you owe, which may include any finance charges that have accumulated and any minimum payments you missed while you were questioning the bill. You then have the time usually given on your type of account to pay any balance.

3. If you still are not satisfied, you should notify the creditor in writing within the time allowed to pay your bill.

MAINTAINING YOUR CREDIT RATING

A creditor may not threaten your credit rating while

you're resolving a billing dispute. Once you have written about a possible error, a creditor is prohibited from giving out information to other creditors or credit bureaus that would damage your credit reputation. And, until your complaint is answered, the creditor also may not take any action to collect the disputed amount.

After the creditor has explained the bill, you may be reported as delinquent on the amount in dispute, and the creditor may take action to collect if you do not pay in the time allowed. Even so, you can still disagree in writing. Then the creditor must report that you have challenged your bill and give you the name and address of each person who has received information about your account. When the matter is settled, the creditor must report the outcome to each person who has received information. Remember that you may also place your own side of the story in your credit record.

DEFECTIVE GOODS OR SERVICES

Your new sofa arrives with only three legs. You try to return it; no luck. You ask the merchant to repair or replace it; still no luck. The Fair Credit Billing Act provides that you may withhold payment on any damaged or poor-quality services purchased with a credit card, as long as you have made a real attempt to solve the problem with the merchant.

This right may be limited if the card was a bank or travel-and-entertainment card or any card not issued by the store where you made your purchase. In such cases, the sale must have been for more than $50 and must have taken place in your home state or within 100 miles of your home address.

CREDIT FOR PAYMENTS AND REFUNDS

If you can avoid finance charges on your account by

paying within a certain period of time, it is obviously important that you receive your bills and get credit for paying them promptly. Check your statements to make sure your creditor follows these rules:

1. *Prompt billing.* Look at the date on the postmark. If your account is one on which no finance or other charge is added before a certain due date, then creditors must mail their statements at least fourteen days before payment is due.

2. *Prompt crediting.* Look at the payment date entered on the statement. Creditors must credit payments on the day they arrive, as long as you follow payment instructions.

3. *Credit balances.* If a credit balance is created on your account (e.g., because you pay more than the amount owed, or you return an item and the purchase price is credited to your account), the creditor must make a refund to you in cash. The refund must be made within seven business days after your written request or automatically if the credit balance is still in existence after six months.

SAMPLE LETTER OF BILLING
ERROR NOTIFICATION

(Your Address)
(Date)

(Company Name)
Credit Department
Street Address
City, State, ZIP

Sir or Madam:

In my most recent billing statement dated _____ (date), I
believe that there is an error. The statement lists a _____
(amount) charge for _____ (item purchased) purchased on_____ (date). I did not make such a
purchase. Please check your records again. My account number is
_____ (account number), and the account is under the
name of _____ (your name).

Thank you for your cooperation.

Sincerely,

(Your Name)

CHAPTER 2

Bills, Bills, Bills: Late Payments and Debt Collectors

IF A CREDITOR HAS RECEIVED NO PAYMENT by the end of the billing cycle, it considers an account delinquent. The initial contact will come in the form of a friendly reminder. This reminder is usually printed on the following month's (billing cycle's) statement or sometimes in a separate letter. Most delinquencies are paid after this reminder. Most people who fall in this category do so because they forgot, misplaced the statement, or are temporarily short of funds.

When no payment has been received during the past two billing cycles, a creditor must be careful in its approach. It wants to keep you as a customer, but it needs to collect the overdue amount. At this stage, you will receive several formal letters about ten to twenty days apart. If no payment or response arrives, the next step is a phone call. A person in the collection department will inform you of the seriousness of the delinquency and inquire as to when you will make a payment.

After about three months of not receiving a payment, the creditor will realize it has a serious problem with the account and will use a stronger approach. Prior to turning the account over to a collection agency or attorney, the creditor will make every effort to contact you and get you to pay. It realizes the longer a debt is overdue, the harder it is to collect.

Next, the company will rescind any credit you may still have available with it, and you will be advised that your account is being handed over to an agency or attorney for collection. In many cases, the firm will charge off your account and write it off as a loss. In some cases, it may have its in-house collection department pursue the debt. If the collection agency is unsuccessful and the amount owed warrants it, the account is given to an attorney for legal action.

THE FAIR DEBT COLLECTION PRACTICES ACT

Congress passed the Fair Debt Collection Practices Act (FDCPA) to protect consumers against harassment and other unethical practices by those who collect unpaid debts. If you are contacted by a debt collector on behalf of one of your creditors, you should be aware of your rights.

Under this law, debt collectors may not use any false or deceptive tactics to collect a debt or obtain information. The following are examples of conduct forbidden by debt collectors when collecting debt:

1. Using a false name
2. Pretending to be a government official, attorney, or credit bureau employee
3. Falsely claiming that you have committed a crime and will be arrested
4. Claiming your wages or property will be seized, unless it is legal and the debt collector or creditor intends to seize your wages or property
5. Giving you papers that appear to be government or legal documents but are not
6. Leading you to believe falsely that certain legal forms

20

do not require any action on your part

7. Giving or threatening to give out false information about you

8. Threatening to take any action that cannot legally be taken or that they do not intend to take

DEBTORS' RIGHTS AT WORK

Working and debt collection don't mix. Whatever your reasons for not paying your debts, you have the right to keep your private financial affairs from becoming common office knowledge. Harassment at work or any place else is illegal. However, it's not illegal for a debt collector to call you at work, unless it's inconvenient for you.

If you tell a collector it's inconvenient for you to receive calls at work, he or she can't call you anymore. Any collector who calls to discuss payment of your debt after you've said not to is breaking the law.

Collectors can, however, contact you to tell you that no further collection efforts will be made or to inform you of a specific action to be taken against you. Or, if the creditor has actually taken court action against you and the court has ordered that your wages be attached (garnished), your employer will have to know. Otherwise, it's no one's business but yours and the debt collector's.

Collectors can call people in your office to try to locate you. In a "locator" call, a collector may only give his or her name and the purpose of the call—to confirm your work and home addresses and home phone number. Locator calls usually can be made only once and cannot indicate that you owe money.

To further protect you, the law says that collectors cannot use postcards to reach you, and they can't use envelopes that indicate that the sender is in the debt-collection business.

In fact, the FDCPA prevents debt collectors from telling your boss or co-workers you owe money, unless you say it's all right, a court says it's all right or such an announcement is part of a court judgment.

If you feel you've been the victim of debt-collection harassment on the job, follow these steps:

1. Tell the caller not to telephone you or anyone at your office or job.

2. Follow up with a letter saying the same thing. It's a good idea to send the letter by certified mail with a return receipt requested. Keep a copy for your files.

3. Make a list of all calls received by you or others after that time, what was said, the general tone, how you responded, and anything else worth noting. Also, save any message slips from debt-collection messages left for you. These will be helpful if you have to take legal action later.

4. If the calls continue, report the matter to your state and local consumer-protection offices and to the Federal Trade Commission, Debt Collection, Washington, D.C. 20580.

5. You might wish to consult an attorney about taking legal action against the debt collector. If you can't afford to hire an attorney, you may qualify for free legal services from a local legal-aid program. Otherwise, your local bar association's lawyer referral service may be able to recommend a private lawyer qualified to handle your case.

If a debt collector violates the FDCPA, you have the right to sue for actual damages, additional damages (up to $1,000), court costs, and reasonable attorney's fees. If you sue, try to find an attorney who is willing to accept whatever the judge awards as the entire fee for representing you.

SAMPLE LETTER REQUESTING COLLECTOR TO END FURTHER COMMUNICATION

(Your Address)
(Date)

Collection Company
Street Address
City, State, ZIP

Sir or Madam:

As I discussed with you on the telephone last week, I maintain that I do not owe the alleged debt to_____ (creditor). Therefore, I wish to end all communication with you, any of your employees, or anyone hired by your company in regard to this alleged debt.

Sincerely,

(Your Signature)

HEARINGS AND COURT JUDGMENTS

If you have received a notice to appear in court concerning a problem with a creditor, it is definitely to your advantage to appear. A creditor must notify you in advance of its intended court action, thus allowing you an opportunity to appear and defend your rights. You have the right to a legal hearing before a creditor can garnish your wages or have your property seized.

Most creditors win judgments simply because the individuals against whom the actions are made do not show up in court. If you do appear, most courts will work with you, and they will often allow an extended period of time for you to repay the account. If you do not appear for the hearing, expect a wage garnishment to be placed in effect.

There are many cases where people have defaulted for valid reasons. Many of these reasons will hold up in court when you have a dispute against the creditor. Such reasons may include defective merchandise, negligent service, improper billing, or fraud. Under the Fair Credit Billing Act, you have the right to withhold payment in any disputed portion of a billing until the creditor resolves the dispute.

Remember, if a creditor informs you that it intends to repossess the articles in dispute, you should:

1. Seek help before you are led to legal proceedings.
2. Always appear at any scheduled hearings.
3. Seek legal assistance through an attorney or your local Legal Aid Society if you need help to defend your case.

CHAPTER 3

The Check Is in the Mail!

AARON PURCHASED A NEW STEREO SYSTEM for $975. Three months later he was laid off his job. His income went from $35,000 a year to unemployment benefits of $3,600 over six months and then ran out entirely. He was a responsible person, but there was no way he could manage to maintain the stereo payments during this crisis. Aaron finally got another job. When he explained his situation and that he wanted desperately to remove the negative mark on his credit record, the company's credit manager agreed to settle the debt for $525. Aaron took the letter he got in exchange and sent it to the local credit bureau. The bureau reinvestigated the item and marked it as paid in full.

This technique is often successful with managers of finance companies. Because of the high turnover, they are usually eager to establish a record of having collected money on accounts that were already written off.

When you negotiate this kind of repayment plan with a creditor, avoid signing anything or making any kind of payments until you obtain a written agreement to correct any negative information on your credit report. Be sure to talk with someone who is in a position to make these kinds of decisions, such as a credit manager or vice president. Also, be sure that you can meet all the requirements on your end of the agreement. Once you agree to pay a debt that was written off, your account may be reactivated. This opens the door for your creditor to begin collection proceedings once again, including lawsuits, if you fail to comply with the agreement.

Let's say you had a debt of $500 that you were unable to pay and the creditor could not collect from you in any way. Eventually this debt was written off as a loss and reported to the credit bureau as a charge-off. Your first step is to budget your income and try to save $300. This is the amount you will use in an effort to negotiate with the creditor.

After you have saved the $300, get in touch with the creditor and tell him how much you regret the bad debt and the negative credit rating, and that you now wish to make amends. When you are talking to the creditor, be sure to give the impression that you still have nothing collectible with which to pay the debt. You do, however, have access to $300 that you would like to use in payment of the $500 debt in exchange for a corrected entry to the credit bureau indicating that the debt has been paid in full.

Remember that you have the bargaining power at this point. The money you are now offering is money the creditor never expected to receive. Since it is like new money coming in, he usually will be willing to negotiate.

If the creditor agrees to your proposal, ask that he sign a statement showing that the $300 is being accepted as payment in full for the $500 debt and that the write-off is no longer in effect. Send this letter to the local credit reporting agency and ask it to restore your positive credit rating.

SAMPLE NEGOTIATED SETTLEMENT LETTER

Address
Date

Name of Creditor
Address
RE: Account

ATT:

The purpose of this letter is to confirm our previous telephone conversation on _____ (date) regarding the settlement of the above account. In accordance with our agreement on the telephone, I will pay your company the amount of $ _____ (amount agreed on) as full settlement of this account. Upon the receipt of the above consideration, your company has agreed to change the remark on my credit file to "paid satisfactorily." In addition, any references to late payment or charge-off regarding this account will be deleted from my credit file.

Your cooperation in this matter is greatly appreciated. If this settlement agreement is acceptable to your company, please so acknowledge with your signature in the space provided below and return a copy to me. Upon receipt of this signed acknowledgment, I will immediately forward you a cashier's check in the amount stated above.

Thank you very much for your immediate attention to this matter.

_____   _____
(Signature of authorized officer)   (Date)

Yours sincerely,

Your Name

CHAPTER 4

*Guerrilla Tactics
for Rapid Debt
Reduction*

THE FOLLOWING IS A LIST OF TACTICS that will allow you to break out of the cycle of increasing debt quickly:

1. Practice abstinence by not incurring additional unsecured debt. (Unsecured debt is any debt that is not secured by some type of collateral, such as a car, house, etc.) Begin by taking all of your credit cards out of your wallet and putting them in a safe place. (The safest place is cut up into little pieces in an envelope en route to the companies that issued them.)

2. Join a support group, such as Debtors Anonymous, and attend meetings on a regular basis. Here you can learn how others overcame their problems with debt and share their experience, strength, and hope.

3. Contact the nearest office of Consumer Credit Counselors and ask for help in developing a repayment plan. They can assist you in drawing up a budget and arranging more lenient repayment schedules.

4. Maintain records of your daily expenses and of the retirement of any portions of your outstanding debts. This will clarify your spending patterns.

5. Make a list of all of the people you owe and arrange to complete your agreements with them all. Resolve to face your responsibilities and to become debt-free.

6. Reduce your outstanding debts to a minimum. Start with the accounts with the lowest balances. Pay them off as soon as possible. Pay off all of your existing debts as soon as you can by making accelerated payments.

7. Find a way to increase your income. This can be done by renting out a room in your home, finding another job, or starting a profitable sideline that requires little start-up capital and minimum overhead.

8. Maintain awareness of the credit system by taking note of bank, loan company, and credit card advertising and by reading news accounts of its effects. Continue to educate yourself by reading other books on consumer credit. Know your rights!

CREATIVE AUTO FINANCING YOUR DEALER NEVER TOLD YOU ABOUT

Before even trying out the latest models, do your homework. Determine the payments you can afford based on your present budget. Then decide on the type of car that fits your particular needs as well as your pocketbook.

One suggestion is to take the monthly payment you expect to pay on the new car and put it in your savings account for six months. See if you can handle the payments, and, if you can with no problem, use what you've saved for the down payment.

You should also try to sell your present vehicle yourself. You can get as much as 25 percent more for it than the dealer will give you. However, do not keep your old car after the day you buy the new one, even if the dealer isn't going to give you the amount you think it is worth. It is more important to lower the amount you must borrow on the new car than it is to get the most you can for the old one.

In financing your new car, be sure that the credit plan allows for early payoff without penalty. Most manufacturers' finance plans are relatively inflexible. They can even have hidden penalties for early payoff or any modification of your terms. Always keep in mind that no matter how low the manufacturer's advertised interest rate is, you will always get a better deal if you can pay cash.

Use all your trade-in money, as well as all the cash you can possibly come up with. Use all the dealer-incentive money you can get and go to your bank or credit union for your financing. Tell your bank representative that your purpose is to pay off your loan as rapidly as possible. Insist that your loan terms allow early payoff. Ask if it is possible to borrow the entire amount you plan to finance for ninety days, promising to refinance the balance into a monthly payment plan at the end of that time.

This time allows you to add as much as you can to your down payment. During this period, work as much overtime as possible, have some garage sales, or sell some unnecessary asset to gather more cash. This can be a special time in which the whole family gets involved in a ninety-day pay-down marathon. If everyone pitches in, it is possible to lower the financed amount by as much as one-half.

Any additional down-payment money you make during this time should be paid to the bank as soon as you get it. Every cent you pay during this period lowers your interest cost from that day on. At the end of that time, refinance the remaining balance for the shortest time possible.

RAPID MORTGAGE REDUCTION

One simple way to reduce the balance on your mortgage

is to make the first loan payment on the day you take out the loan. If the first payment is made on the day the loan is made, many months, and possibly even several years, can be reduced from the total length of your mortgage.

Here's how it works. In the first years of the mortgage, only a very small percentage of your monthly payment goes toward the principal. The majority of your payment goes toward paying interest. If the first payment is made on the day you make your loan, there is no interest due at that time. The entire payment will be subtracted from the principal of the loan.

Another way to pay off your mortgage rapidly is to make a payment every week. To figure the amount that each weekly payment should be, multiply your monthly payment times twelve (months in a year), then divide that amount by fifty-two (weeks in a year). The answer will give you the amount your weekly payment should be.

Let's say, for example, that your mortgage payment is $866.67 per month. If you multiply that by twelve months, you have the amount of your total annual mortgage payment. Your answer will be $10,400. Now divide $10,400 by fifty-two weeks. Your answer will be $200. If you then pay $200 each week, you will drastically lower the amount of interest you owe.

Each week you will be lowering the principal and interest by a small amount. At first it won't seem like you're accomplishing much, but by the time several years have passed, the savings will become more significant. The interest on a mortgage that is paid off weekly will be lowered by as much as 60 percent when compared to a similar mortgage that is paid off with monthly payments. Not only will the total interest cost be less, but the time it takes to pay off the mortgage will be drastically reduced if this procedure is followed faithfully.

Another alternative is to make a half-payment every fourteen days. This will result in making one extra payment each year and will take years off the length of time it takes to pay off the balance of your mortgage. If a half-payment is made every two weeks, you will make twenty-six half-payments each year. Fifty-two weeks divided by two weeks equals twenty-six weeks. Divide the twenty-six half-payments by two, and you have thirteen full payments instead of the twelve you would make if you paid one full payment each month.

These suggestions are all mathematically sound methods of rapid mortgage reduction. But remember that any modification made to an existing mortgage must be approved by the lender. The mortgage holder is not obligated to do anything that is not expressly stated in the loan agreement that you both signed. It is best to make these types of arrangements before you take out the mortgage. However, many lenders will agree to modify your payment schedule if you ask.

THE TRUTH ABOUT DEBT CONSOLIDATION

A consolidation loan will rarely reduce the amount of money you owe. There will be new loan costs to add to your balance. Your interest costs will also go up because you will be taking much longer to pay off the new loan. Consolidation borrowing almost always adds to the total debt. In other words, you can't borrow your way out of debt.

Let's imagine that your current bills total $10,000, and it will take five years to pay off a consolidation loan at a payment of $265 per month. With this loan structure, your new debt, with interest, equals $15,900. If you earn $10 an hour, that means you are sentencing yourself to 1,590 hours of work to pay off the total obligation.

The act of debt consolidation usually results in a somewhat lower monthly payment, but this payment must be made for a much longer period of time. For example, you could also consolidate that same $10,000 debt so that your payments would drop to half the $265 we used in the previous illustration. This would make your new payment only $132.50 per month.

Sounds great, doesn't it? Think about it, though. The term of the lower monthly payment will now be twelve years instead of five years. So, your true total debt will go up to $19,080, and, at $10 an hour, the time it will take you to pay off that new, easy payment consolidation loan is 1,908 hours.

In the process of consolidating your debt, you have increased the sentence you must serve to pay off that debt by 318 precious hours of your income-producing life.

Consolidation by a bank or finance company usually will not reduce your total cost in terms of time served to pay off your debt. These institutions almost always charge a higher interest rate because your risk of default or bankruptcy has increased since you made the original loans.

Debt consolidation is simply another method of enslaving you in further debt. The lender is the one who benefits, not the borrower. Debt consolidation is done for three basic reasons:

1. It discourages bankruptcies.
2. It gives the lender a chance to adjust the interest rate upward.
3. The lender has the opportunity to add collateral to the loan.

Once again, you can't borrow your way out of debt—no matter what the commercials might lead you to believe. You can only borrow your way deeper into debt.

The only exception is if you can get the interest on your total bill reduced. This will cause the debt to be paid off more quickly because more of each payment will be going toward paying off the balance of your loan. Usually the only circumstance in which this can happen is when you owe large amounts of high-interest credit card debts. They can sometimes be consolidated into a second mortgage on your home, which usually carries a lower interest rate. This type of loan can also have the additional advantage of being tax-deductible.

LAST-RESORT STRATEGIES

If you feel your back is to the wall but not quite enough to file bankruptcy, write your creditors and propose a more favorable alternative. You can often obtain many favorable terms by simply threatening to file bankruptcy. The credit manager who was on your back will suddenly become a model of generosity, offering temporary collection moratoria, extended payments—anything at all to get more return on the credit his company extended than what the bankruptcy court will give him. Ask for a debt moratorium to help you get back on your feet and resume payments at a later time, or suggest reducing payments to an amount you can reasonably handle. The cost of fighting a bankruptcy petition, along with the near certainty of having little or nothing to show for it, should make most creditors ready to agree to your proposal.

SAMPLE LETTER TO REQUEST A MORATORIUM

RE: Account and amount due

Dear Credit Manager:

I have carefully reviewed my financial condition, and I find that it is impossible for me to meet the scheduled monthly payments on my indebtedness to you. (List special reason for present hardship, e.g., emergency expenses, large medical bills, unemployment.)

After deducting my carefully budgeted living expenses from my current monthly income, the balance is simply inadequate to pay my debts at the present rate. Therefore,

(Alternative 1)

I propose that my payments be reduced to $ _____ (amount) next year, unless the debt is paid off sooner. Payments of $ _____ (amount) are within my means and will be made regularly.

(Alternative 2)

I propose a ____-month (specify length) moratorium on my repayment of my debt. At the end of that period, I hope to resume monthly payments of $ _____ (amount) per month, for at least _____ (specify) months.

Your cooperation will be of considerable help in avoiding the alternative of bankruptcy.

Sincerely,

Your Name

SAMPLE REQUEST FOR
REDUCED MONTHLY PAYMENTS

Name of Creditor
Address
City, State, ZIP

RE: Account #

Dear Credit Manager:

If you check my account, you will find that I am delinquent in payment. I have been trying my best to pay my debt to you since being laid off work in January. With a 30-percent rent increase and the rising cost of food, all my unemployment benefits go toward supporting my family.

I would like to have your consent to a repayment plan that is realistic and manageable for me. My present balance is $400. With your consent, I will be sending you a payment of $20 each month, starting 1 June 1993. Payment in full would be in approximately twenty months instead of the present ten months. With this manageable payment plan, I foresee no circumstances that would prevent me from making these payments. A check in the amount of $20 is enclosed. Please notify me if you find these terms acceptable, and I will come in to sign a contract.

My family and I have always valued a good credit standing and, therefore, would like to take all necessary steps to preserve a good standing.

Thank you for your patience and confidence. I will increase my payments whenever my budget allows.

Sincerely yours,

Your Name

CHAPTER 5

Going Bankrupt without Going Broke

After twelve years of marriage, Jennifer's husband disappeared, leaving her to care for five children. He also left her with $63,000 in outstanding loans and mortgage payments. After two years of trying to make ends meet, Jennifer sought protection under Chapter 7 of the bankruptcy code.

"Filing bankruptcy seemed like my only way out," Jennifer said. "I tried to establish credit and pay off my bills by myself, but I just couldn't make it. When my husband left and stopped making child-support payments, I just couldn't do it anymore."

People who file for bankruptcy are usually struggling to get by with the basic necessities of life. They are not living lavishly, running up big bills, and then filing for bankruptcy to avoid responsibility. If income is disrupted for any length of time because of injury, sickness, or layoff, even the most comfortable among us can suddenly find ourselves swimming in a sea of credit card debts, medical bills, and overdue rent or mortgage payments. For some people, bankruptcy can offer a fresh start in life.

The Bankruptcy Act is a federal law that is intended to

benefit both troubled debtors and their creditors. One purpose is to make sure the debtor's property is equitably distributed to the creditors so no creditor will have unfair advantage over the others.

The law also provides the honest debtor with protection against his creditors' demands for payment. If the debtor makes a full and honest accounting of his assets and liabilities and deals fairly with the creditors, he may have most, if not all, of his debts discharged or cancelled. The bankruptcy process is intended to give the debtor a new beginning without the burden of unmanageable debts.

The tradition of debt relief dates back to the time of Moses. To protect the poor, a provision of the Year of Jubilee, celebrated every fifty years, was the cancellation of all private debts incurred by the Israelites. For example, Israelites whose debts had caused them to be sold as slaves were released from debts and given their liberty.

Bankruptcy statutes have been around in England since 1542. The U.S. Constitution provides for bankruptcy legislation. The Bankruptcy Act of 1898 formed the basis of U.S. laws for many years. Congress completely revised the act in 1978 and added further amendments in 1984.

CHAPTER 7 LIQUIDATION

There are basically two types of bankruptcy protection for the individual consumer: Chapter 7 liquidation and Chapter 13 debt adjustment. Chapter 7 liquidation, sometimes referred to as straight bankruptcy, is the most common form of bankruptcy filed by debtors.

Under Chapter 7, most of your debts will be discharged by the court, and you never have to repay them. However, certain debts are not dischargeable and will survive bankruptcy. For example, certain income taxes that accrue prior to the filing of a petition and obligations to pay alimony and child support are not dischargeable. You should consult your attorney as to what kinds of debts are dischargeable in your particular case.

The primary purpose of this kind of bankruptcy is to give an honest debtor a fresh start in life without the pressure and discouragement of substantial indebtedness. The result is complete forgiveness of all debts and a chance to rebuild one's life.

Another feature of bankruptcy protection is the *automatic stay*. To relieve the debtor from the financial pressure and the harassment of creditors' collection efforts, the law provides that filing the bankruptcy petition results in an automatic stay to actions against the debtor. This stay stops all collection activities (such as lawsuits employed in the collection efforts of creditors).

Disadvantages of Chapter 7

Chapter 7 bankruptcy is not a panacea for everyone with financial difficulties. It has its limitations, which include:

1. *Frequency*. It cannot be filed again within the next six years

2. *Disposition of assets*. Upon filing the bankruptcy petition, the property belonging to the debtor, with the exception of certain property exempted under federal or state laws, becomes part of the debtor's estate to be liquidated for distribution to creditors. Therefore, the loss of assets must be considered when contemplating the filing of a petition.

CHAPTER 13 DEBT ADJUSTMENT

An alternative to Chapter 7 liquidation is Chapter 13 debt adjustment. Formerly known as the "Wage Earner Plan,"

Chapter 13 is designed to enable individual debtors to apply a portion of their debts over an extended period of time. This is done under court supervision and through a court-appointed trustee. The debtor is protected from the creditors by an automatic stay, while a plan of repayment is developed and carried out.

The underlying policy is to encourage debtors to pay their debts instead of merely seeking a discharge. Therefore, the justification of pursuing Chapter 13 relief instead of liquidation is one of moral consideration. For many debtors, however, this sense of morality often creates a difficult course to pursue because of the need to support dependents while being burdened by the repayment of heavy debts. Many of those who file under Chapter 13 with good intentions can never follow through with the payment plan and finally abandon it. As a result, the case is dismissed under the petition of the trustee or converted to Chapter 7.

Advantages of Chapter 13

1. Chapter 13 protects the debtor's nonexempt assets, which would be lost in a liquidation case. Thus, it is important for you to consult an attorney and determine the extent of your property that is nonexempt and its value.

2. If there are substantial nondischargeable debts, such as spousal support, student loans, or willful and malicious injury to property, Chapter 13 allows you to eliminate, reduce, or pay such debts over an extended period of time. In contrast, a Chapter 7 liquidation would not protect the debtor from enforcement of these nondischargeable obligations.

3. Chapter 13 is available to individuals who may not be eligible for a Chapter 7 discharge. For example, a person who received a discharge under Chapter 7 within the past six years can't obtain another discharge under it but may seek relief and receive one under Chapter 13.

4. A debtor's personal sense of morality may compel him to file under Chapter 13 and lessen the sense of guilt. Chapter 13 allows an individual to maintain a sense of integrity.

5. Future creditors may look favorably upon a person who, despite past financial failures, has attempted to repay his/her debts in an honest and ethical way.

6. The new Chapter 13 code contains a special automatic stay provision applicable to co-debtors or cosigners. After the filing of a Chapter 13 case, a creditor may not act on, commence, or continue any civil action to collect all or any part of the debt from any individual who is liable with the debtor. The stay also protects any individuals who put up collateral to secure the debt. However, it is important to understand that this stay would not affect the substantive rights of the lender with respect to the cosigner's liability. All it does is require the lender to wait for payment under the Chapter 13 plan before pursuing remedies against the co-debtor.

7. The filing of Chapter 13 stops interest charges on your accounts.

Tamara and her husband, John, opened a restaurant catering to upscale customers in the entertainment industry. John had experience in the restaurant industry and had researched the market well, so they had big dreams of success.

As partners, Tamara and John agreed to invest an equal amount in the business. Tamara's half came from her grandmother in Oregon, who was entering a retirement home. Quite wealthy at the time, her grandmother agreed to sell her home and give Tamara the proceeds for her stake in the restaurant. John told Tamara his half would come from a friend in Texas, a silent partner.

The restaurant was opened with great fanfare and did well for several months. However, as Tamara recalls, "We were overstaffed and undercapitalized. Most celebrities opted for trendier establishments, and our cash-flow problems increased. After a year or so, we had to borrow money to stay afloat. We used our personal friends, and even my parents and an uncle signed personal notes."

Eventually Tamara realized that John had not invested any money in the business. "No wonder we were having problems," she lamented. We just went broke and filed bankruptcy. The bank that owned our fixtures advised us to hold a bankruptcy sale. Our employees were loyal to the end and even offered to work without paychecks.

"It seems everything fell apart at the same time, including my marriage. I know the marriage could have worked out if it hadn't been for the bankruptcy. John was so depressed he could hardly function. His dream had been destroyed, and he couldn't cope with the consequences. I felt sorry for him, but I also felt betrayed because he never put money into the business. He lied to me."

Tamara says that many of their so-called friends regarded them as "deadbeats" and no longer wanted to associate with them. Their children were ridiculed at school. Tamara couldn't get credit anywhere and even had trouble getting a check cashed.

Tamara managed to pay off the loans guaranteed by her parents and her uncle. However, family members, including her mother, treated her coolly. Since Tamara's grandmother spent her final years (and her fortune) in a retirement home, Tamara was the only family member to get any of her money. And it was all gone.

With children to support and educate, Tamara's life was difficult. But she was determined not to let these reverses ruin their lives. She went back to work and, with the help of a financial counselor, reestablished her credit.

Today she is the president of her own consulting firm.

Her work brings her in contact with people having financial problems. "They often say to me, 'You just don't know what it's like to be so heavily in debt.'"

"Oh yes, I do," Tamara assures them, "but there is life after debt."

WHERE TO GET HELP

Debtors Anonymous is an effective support group for anyone with a debt or spending problem. It is based on the twelve steps of Alcoholics Anonymous, and there are no dues or fees. To get a meeting list or help in forming a chapter in your area, contact: Debtors Anonymous, P.O. Box 20322, New York, NY 10025-9992. In Los Angeles contact: D.A., 10880 Wilshire Blvd., 19th Floor, Los Angeles, CA 90024.

The National Foundation for Consumer Credit has 245 offices around the country. For the location nearest you, contact NFCC, 8701 Georgia Avenue, Silver Spring, MD 20910 . Also known as **Consumer Credit Counselors,** they can help you arrange a realistic budget and negotiate with your creditors. Check your phone book under Consumer Credit Counselors for the location nearest you.

The Family Service Association of America is another source of help for people with debt problems. This organization has branches nationwide, and fees may vary based on your locale and income. For more information write: 44 E. 23rd Street, New York, NY 10010.

PART TWO

*A Do-It-Yourself
Guide to Credit
Repair*

CHAPTER 6

How Do You Rate?
Credit-Reporting
Agencies

DAVID DIDN'T NOTICE WHEN THE CREDIT CARD BILLS first started falling behind. Sarah was in charge of paying bills. He was shocked, however, when he discovered the check for his student loan payment was returned for non-sufficient funds.

"The bank must have made a mistake," Sarah insisted. "Don't worry about it, honey. I'll take care of it."

The marriage was showing strains of the couple's over-spending. Their credit cards were charged beyond their limits, David's student loan was two months past due, the checking account was overdrawn, and their savings had long since been depleted.

When his wife filed for divorce, David was left with mountains of bills, including an overdue student loan. His car payment was two months late, and his checking account was $700 overdrawn. Creditors threatened to sue and garnish his wages.

On the advice of his attorney, David filed for protection under Chapter 13 of the bankruptcy code. The automatic stay gave him enough breathing room to begin getting his life back in order.

49

Three years later, David completed his debt repayment plan and was ready to start over again in the credit world. Much wiser now, he knew that he would never make the same mistakes he had made before. With a good job and steady income, David decided that it was time to purchase a new car. The 1978 Volvo he had been driving was costing him more money in repairs than he would be paying for a new car loan. To his surprise and humiliation, he was denied credit at every place he applied.

One of the car dealers referred David to a credit-repair company. The company promised that for $700 it would erase the negative information from his credit file and help him rebuild his credit rating. Three months after paying to have his credit restored, David discovered the company had disappeared. His credit rating was still the same. He had been one of thousands of victims who had been lured into the trap of easy answers and promises that are too good to be true.

For years, the Federal Trade Commission, Better Business Bureau, Consumer Credit Counselors, and Associated Credit Bureaus, Inc., have warned consumers to beware of unscrupulous operators in the credit-repair industry. Despite such efforts, however, consumers have consistently beaten a pathway to the door of every new credit-repair company that has sprung up. The fees for these services often range from $100 to $1,200. The biggest complaint is that consumers sometimes receive little or no results from these companies, which sometimes go out of business within a few months.

According to Ken Yarbrough, Executive Director of the Consumer Credit Commission, there are approximately 100 credit-repair companies in the United States. Approximately 70 million consumers are in need of such services. Here's the dilemma: a recent study by Consolidated Information Services, Inc., an independent credit bureau based in New

Jersey, revealed a 47-percent error factor in reporting factual information on credit reports. Clearly, American consumers are in need of help.

This book offers a low-cost alternative to the high-cost, high-risk services offered by the credit-repair companies. It is based on proven strategies used by attorneys and professional credit consultants to "erase bad credit" from your files and help you to get a new start in life. It doesn't matter what your present situation is. All you need is a willingness to learn a few basic concepts and to put those concepts into action.

CREDIT RATINGS

As you know, we live in a credit-oriented society. Most stores won't even accept a personal check without a major credit card to back it up. It is almost impossible to buy a house or a car without obtaining some type of financing. Even renting an apartment takes good credit these days.

Negative information in your credit files, such as previous late payments, collection accounts, or judgments can prevent a lender from even considering your credit application . . . regardless of your ability to pay.

In other cases, it can result in higher interest rates and extra finance charges (known as "points"). This can mean a difference of several thousand dollars on a large credit purchase, such as a new car or home.

In light of this reality, it is imperative that you begin now to improve your credit rating. If you're like 70 percent of American consumers, you probably have at least one item of negative information in your credit bureau files. In many cases, the information is incorrect, misleading, inaccurate, or obsolete. Perhaps your file contains information about someone else with a similar name or Social Security number. One of the major credit bureaus has published so much incorrect information that rumor has it their initials are an acronym for The Report's Wrong!

Credit bureaus, also known as credit-reporting agencies, make money by compiling and selling information about you that has been reported to them by subscribers. These subscribers include banks, department stores, finance companies, collection agencies, and mortgage companies. The information includes credit histories, account balances, and payment patterns.

The credit bureaus also receive and report information found in public records. This includes bankruptcies, judgments, tax liens, wage garnishments, and notices of default. Public-record information is generally gathered manually, which can lead to inaccurate information being reported in your file.

What the Report Really Says: Positive, Neutral, and Negative Notations

The information in your credit report is usually divided into three types of ratings: positive, neutral, and negative.

The following are the only statements in your credit report that are considered *positive*:

1. Paid satisfactorily or paid as agreed
2. Current account with no late payments
3. Account/credit line closed at consumer's request

The following notations are considered *neutral*, but in reality, anything less than a positive rating is considered negative by many credit grantors:

1. Paid, was 30 days late
2. Current, was 30 days late
3. Inquiry

4. Credit card lost
5. Refinance
6. Settled
7. Paid

The following are considered *negative*:

1. Bankruptcy—Chapter 7 or Chapter 13
2. Judgments
3. Tax liens
4. Account closed—grantor's request
5. Paid, was 60, 90, or 120 days late
6. SCNL (subscriber cannot locate)
7. Paid, collection
8. Paid, charge-off
9. Bk liq reo (bankruptcy liquidation)
10. Charge-off
11. Collection account
12. Delinquent
13. Current, was 60, 90, or 120 days late
14. CHECKPOINT, TRANS ALERT, or CAUTION (potential fraud indicators)
15. Excessive inquiries (looks like you've been turned down by everyone else).

THE FIVE LARGEST CREDIT BUREAUS

The following are the addresses to write or phone numbers to call, to request a copy of your credit report.

TRW Credit Data/National Consumer Relations Center
12606 Greenville Avenue/P.O. Box 749029
Dallas, TX 75374-9029
(214) 235-1200 ext. 251

Equifax
P.O. Box 4081
Atlanta, GA 30302

Trans Union
East
P.O. Box 360
Philadelphia, PA 19105
(215) 569-4582
Midwest
Consumer Relations
222 S. First Street, Ste. 201
Louisville, KY 40202
(502) 584-0121
West
P.O. Box 3110
Fullerton, CA 92634
(714) 738-3800

The Associated Credit Bureaus, a trade organization, offers a free brochure called "Consumers, Credit Bureaus and the Fair Reporting Act."

Write:
Associated Credit Bureaus, Inc.
1090 Vermont Avenue
N.W., Ste. 200
Washington, D.C. 20005-4905

QUESTIONS AND ANSWERS ABOUT CREDIT-REPORTING AGENCIES

Q: What is a credit-reporting agency?

A: A credit-reporting agency is commonly called a credit bureau. A credit bureau is a business organization that puts together a report about your past credit performance, keeps the information up-to-date, and, for a fee, furnishes the information in the form of credit reports to merchants, credit card issuers, insurance companies, and potential employers.

Q: Do I have the right to know what is in my credit file?

A: Under the Fair Credit Reporting Act, all consumers have the right to know what is in their credit files at credit bureaus.

Q: What type of information is contained in my credit file?

A: Your credit file contains several different types of information:

1. Identifying information, such as your name, address and Social Security number
2. Information concerning your current employment, such as the position you hold, the length of your employment, and your income
3. Information about your personal history, such as your date of birth, number of dependents, previous addresses, and previous employment
4. Information about your credit history, such as how promptly you made payments to previous creditors
5. Information about you that is available publicly, such as records of arrests, indictments, convictions, lawsuits, tax liens, marriages, bankruptcies, and court judgments

Q: Who may obtain a copy of my credit file?

A: Only someone with a legitimate business need may see your credit file. Your credit file may be disclosed only to someone the credit bureau believes will use the information for one or more of the following purposes:

1. Granting you credit, reviewing your account, or collecting on your account
2. Considering you for possible employment
3. Considering you for an insurance policy
4. Deciding whether or not you are eligible for a license or other government-related benefits, which by law require consideration of your financial responsibility or status. A credit bureau may also disclose "identifying" information, such as your name, address, places of employment, and former places of employment to a government agent.
5. Furnishing information for a business transaction between you and another person, such as renting an apartment, as long as the person requesting the report has a legitimate need for the information
6. Responding to a court order
7. Responding to an Internal Revenue Service (IRS) subpoena (with IRS notification and ample time for you to challenge the subpoena)

Your credit file may also be disclosed to someone if you give your written permission to the credit bureau to disclose your file to that person.

Q: Why should I care about the information in my credit file?

A: The information contained in your credit file often determines whether or not you will be granted credit. It may also be used by insurance companies to decide whether to insure you or to set your insurance rate. Often, incorrect information is entered in your file, and if this occurs, you would want to have it removed.

Q: How can I find out what information is in my credit file?

A: If you applied for credit and were rejected, were denied insurance, or the cost of the insurance increased based on information contained in a credit report, the creditor denying you credit or insurance is required by law to supply you with the name and address of the credit bureau that supplied the report.

The credit bureau is required to disclose the information it has about you free of charge if you ask for the disclosure within thirty days of being notified of your credit or insurance denial. You can get in touch with the credit bureau either in person, by letter, or by telephone to learn what is in your credit file.

If you are simply curious to know what is in your file, you can contact a credit bureau for that information, but in this case, you will have to pay the credit bureau a fee or service charge. You can find the names of credit bureaus in your area by looking in the yellow pages under the heading of "Credit-Reporting Agencies." If more than one agency is listed, you should contact each one to see if it has your credit report on file.

Q: What is an investigative report, and how is it different from a credit report?

A: An investigative report differs from a standard credit report in two ways:

1. It contains a different kind of information, and the information is gathered in a different way. While a credit report contains information relating to your credit history

and information available from public records, an investigative report deals with matters of a more personal nature, such as your character, general reputation, and life-style.

2. The information in an investigative report comes from personal interviews with your friends, associates, and neighbors, while information in a credit report is obtained directly from the credit bureau and from public records.

Q: What are investigative reports used for?

A: Investigative reports are used mostly by insurance companies and potential employers. Insurance companies use them in helping to decide if you are a good insurance risk. Potential employers may use them to help decide whether they want to hire you. Your current employer may use them to help in deciding on promotions.

Q: Do I have to give my permission before an investigative report can be made about me?

A: No, but the person who requests an investigative report has three days to notify you that an investigative report has been ordered. You have no right, however, to be informed that a report has been ordered if it is to be used for employment positions for which you have not specifically applied.

Q: Can I find out what information is in my investigative file?

A: Yes. You are entitled to know the "nature and substance" of all information in your investigative file. You are *not* entitled to know the source of information if the information was gathered only for use in preparing an investigative report and used for no other purpose. You are also entitled to know who has received investigative reports about you within the past six months, or within the last two years if the report was made for employment purposes.

Q: Does the law provide penalties for someone who willfully obtains information from a credit bureau under false pretenses?

A: Yes. Anyone willfully obtaining information from a credit-reporting agency under false pretenses is subject to a maximum criminal fine of $5,000, or a maximum of one year in prison, or both.

Q: Does the law provide any penalties for officers or employees of credit-reporting agencies who willfully provide information from the agency's files to an unauthorized person?

A: Yes. The penalties are the same as above.

Q: If a consumer believes a credit bureau has violated the law but does not want to sue, can he complain to someone?

A: Yes. A consumer can file a complaint with the Federal Trade Commission, state attorney general's office, or local district attorney's office.

CHAPTER 7

*Applying for
Credit*

IN ADDITION TO LOOKING AT YOUR CREDIT REPORT, the prospective lender will evaluate the information supplied on your credit application.

THE FIVE Cs OF CONSUMER CREDIT

A lender will consider five elements, the "five Cs," before extending you credit:

• *Collateral*. What type of security is offered against the loan?
• *Character*. This includes work history, residential information, other accounts, references, etc.
• *Capacity*. This is the ratio of debt to income, or the ability to generate cash flow.
• *Capital*. Net worth or sum of assets minus liabilities.
• *Conditions*. How present economic factors relate to credit availability.

Most creditors use a "point system" to evaluate your application in relation to the above. Various elements of your application are assigned a certain number of points, depending upon how you answer each question. In some cases a "high scoring" application can offset a negative credit history reflected on your credit report. In other instances, a "low scoring" credit application may negate an otherwise excellent credit history. For example, a person with a previous bankruptcy may still be able to obtain credit if he can demonstrate sufficient income, stable job history, long-time residence, and other credit references. On the other hand, a person with an excellent credit report may be denied credit if the application shows that he is new to the area, with a new job and a high debt-to-income ratio. The following is an example of a point-scoring system used by a number of credit grantors, including major banks and department stores:

POINT SCORING SYSTEM

Employment	Points
1 year or less at present employment	0
1-2 years	1
2-4 years	2
5-10 years	3
Over 10 years	4

Income (gross monthly)	
Less than $1,000	0
$1,000 to $1,500	1
$1,500 to $2,000	2
Over $2,000	3

Length at Present Address	
Less than 3 years	0
3 years or more	1

	Points
Savings Account	
No	0
Yes	1
Checking Account	
No	0
Account with this bank, but with five returned items over past year	1
Account with this bank, but with no returned items over past year	2
Previous Loan with this Bank	
No	0
Yes, but still open	0
Yes, but closed with two or fewer late payments	1
Credit References	
No	0
Yes	1
Obligations Past Due	
Yes	0
No	1
Monthly Obligations vs. Income	
50 percent	0
40 percent to 49 percent	1
30 percent to 39 percent	2
Less than 30 percent	3
Own Real Estate	
No	0
Yes	1

Telephone Listed in Applicant's Name	Points
No	0
Yes	1

Age of Automobile

Over one year	0
Less than one year	1

Score

90-100: Loan granted automatically
70-89: Loan granted unless there is a good reason to deny
50-69: Reasonable risk; review application toward approval
40-49: Review application toward rejection
0-39: Reject application automatically

CHAPTER 8

*Special Problems
of Previously
Married People*

AN INCREASING NUMBER OF HOUSEHOLDS are now headed by previously married people. This chapter deals with various credit situations that individuals may encounter when they divorce, separate, or become widowed. Unlike the other chapters in this book, the problems presented here do not focus on any particular federal law. In some instances, credit problems that arise with individuals who were previously married may have to be settled in court. Remember that situations will vary among individuals and among states. Therefore, the answers presented here are general in nature and may not apply to all cases. They should be considered only as a guide to credit problems for previously married individuals.

Q: My husband recently died, and now I find that the credit accounts that were in his name only have been cut off. Can creditors do this even if I have a substantial income from my husband's estate?

A: Yes, if your husband's credit accounts were in his name only, creditors may discontinue your use of them upon his death. You may, however, reapply for credit in your own name.

Q: My wife ran up sizable bills on my credit card at department stores before we were separated. Am I responsible for paying her bills?

A: Yes, if the credit accounts are in your name, you are responsible for the bills. You should, however, notify the creditors, preferably in writing, that your wife is no longer authorized to charge on your accounts. She would then have to open accounts in her name and be considered for credit on her own.

In many states, however, there is an old legal doctrine called "the law of necessaries" that makes a person responsible for certain debts incurred by the spouse, such as bills for food, clothing, and shelter. In some states, obligations under the doctrine cease upon separation, but in other states a spouse can be held liable for necessaries until a divorce decree is entered.

The bills in question would have to be settled between you and your wife should you seek a divorce or some separation that involves a settlement.

Q: My husband left, and now I am receiving calls from his creditors for items that he purchased for his own use. Am I responsible for his bills?

A: If the accounts were in both names, you are also responsible for the bills. If the accounts were in his name only, you would not be responsible for his debts. Should you and your husband separate or divorce, the matter of these debts should be part of your legal settlement.

Q: My spouse and I recently separated. Can I prevent my spouse from using our joint credit cards?

A: If either party of a joint account notifies the creditor that he or she wants to close the account, the creditor will close it. Neither party will then be able to use it. Both spouses can then apply for credit in their own names based upon their creditworthiness. Since the account was a joint account, both spouses are liable for all charges made up to the time the account was closed.

Q: My wife and I recently divorced. I just found out she is continuing to charge on my credit accounts. Am I responsible for paying these bills?

A: Yes, if you did not give notice to the creditors that you no longer allow your ex-wife to charge on your account. Once you notify a creditor that you no longer authorize her to use your account, you are not responsible for the charges she makes.

Q: I am separated from my husband and receive monthly child-support payments from him. Must I disclose these payments when I apply for credit in my own name?

A: No, you don't have to disclose monthly child-support payments. If you decide to disclose them, a creditor who considers income as part of a credit application must consider child-support payments as part of your income if they are made on a regular basis.

Q: Must credit bureaus maintain separate files on me now that I am divorced from my spouse?

A: Yes, credit bureaus must report information about you separately. However, that information may include your credit history on accounts that you held jointly with your spouse prior to your divorce, or information on accounts that were in your spouse's name but authorized for your use.

Q: My former spouse was a poor credit risk and had an unfavorable credit history. Can I be denied credit after we divorce based on information creditors receive about accounts I shared with my ex-spouse?

A: According to the Equal Credit Opportunity Act (ECOA), if you have been denied credit simply because an ex-spouse was a poor credit risk, a creditor must consider any information that you can offer to show that the unfavorable credit history on a former joint account does not accurately reflect your own credit history. In addition, the Fair Credit Reporting Act allows you to include a statement of dispute concerning inaccurate information on your credit report.

Q: After our divorce, my ex-spouse declared bankruptcy. Will that affect my credit rating?

A: Not if the bankruptcy occurred after your divorce. Once you are divorced, the credit history of your ex-spouse would have no effect on your credit standing. The ECOA requires creditors to consider applicants on the basis of their own creditworthiness and not that of their spouses or ex-spouses.

CHAPTER 9

Women, Minorities, and Credit

THE EQUAL CREDIT OPPORTUNITY ACT was enacted by Congress to eliminate discrimination against women seeking to obtain credit. It was expanded to include the prohibition of denying credit based on a person's race, color, place of national origin, religion, sex, age, or marital status. Further, a woman who exercises her rights under the act cannot be "blacklisted" from obtaining credit.

One of the main problems with the ECOA is that it is difficult to prove discrimination since other reasons can be given for denial of credit. Another problem is that the people the law was designed to protect seldom exercise their rights, usually because of one of the following reasons:

1. Since credit rejection may be masqueraded by another reason, the applicant may not even realize she has been a victim of discrimination.

2. Most people don't know their rights under the law and are unaware of the ease of filing a complaint.

3. A woman may feel it is unladylike to raise a fuss.

4. The applicant may not want to get involved with "fighting the system."

5. It may seem easier just to apply somewhere else.

The general rule of thumb to determine whether you have been a victim of discrimination is to ask yourself if you would have been granted the loan if you were a nonminority with the same economic status. The following is a summary of your rights under the ECOA:

• If your income is enough to warrant the loan (sufficient debt-to-income-ratio), the lender cannot require you to get a cosigner or coapplicant.
• If you are a woman, you may use your maiden or married name (whichever you choose). You may even use a combination of both.
• The creditor may inquire as to how many dependents you have to determine your spendable income. However, he cannot ask about your birth-control practices or plans for parenthood.
• The creditor must consider all income derived from alimony, child support, public assistance, and part-time work. A woman is not required to reveal alimony and child support if she chooses not to. (If she chooses not to, then these amounts will not be taken into consideration when computing her debt-to-income-ratio.)
• A woman cannot be denied credit automatically for listing her occupation as a housewife.
• If there is a change in a woman's marital status (divorced, widowed, separated) or she chooses to change her name legally, the creditor cannot automatically require her to reapply for an existing loan. The only exception is if there appears to be a problem with a loan where a former husband's income had been considered at the time the loan was approved.
• A woman's marital status cannot be inquired into if she

70

is trying to obtain separate unsecured credit. The only exception is if the applicant lives in a community property state (Arizona, California, Idaho, Louisiana, Nevada, New Mexico, Texas, and Washington).

SAMPLE COMPLAINT LETTER

Name
Address
City, State, ZIP

Date

Name of Government Agency
City, State, ZIP
Ref: Name of Bank
Address
City, State, ZIP

Account Number:

To Whom It May Concern:

Please accept this letter as a formal complaint about the above-referenced bank. My complaint is as follows:

(Detail the specific violations committed by the bank.)

I have attempted to resolve this issue directly with _____
_____ (name of bank) to no avail. The key person I dealt with was
_____ (name of person and title).
Enclosed are photocopies of all related paperwork to document my claim.

Sincerely yours,

Your Name

CHAPTER 10

Disputing with the Credit Bureaus

THE FEDERAL GOVERNMENT ENACTED the Fair Credit Reporting Act on 25 April 1971 to protect consumers against the reporting of inaccurate, misleading, or obsolete information. Lawmakers designed the law to ensure that consumer-reporting agencies operate in a responsible and equitable manner.

THE FAIR CREDIT REPORTING ACT

The FCRA provides a list of rights and procedures that will assist you in clearing away negative remarks and reestablishing your creditworthiness—regardless of your previous credit history.

By understanding your rights and using the law to your advantage, it is possible to remove bankruptcy, judgments, late payments, collection accounts, charge-offs, and other derogatory information from your files permanently.

The first step is to obtain copies of your credit reports from each of the major credit bureaus in your area. You can find the address of your local credit bureau in the yellow pages under "Credit-Reporting Agencies." If you have been denied credit within the past thirty days, you can obtain a free copy of your report by enclosing a photocopy of the denial letter along with your request. Be sure to include your full name, date of birth, Social Security number, and addresses for the past five years.

If you have not been denied credit within the last thirty days, you may purchase a copy of your report from each credit bureau. In California, for example, the cost for a copy of your report is $8 from each of the major bureaus. The cost may vary in other states.

You also have the right to visit the credit bureau in person to review your file. This can be done by calling the bureau and making an appointment. You will then need to present the proper identification and pay the required fee. The law also allows you to be accompanied by one other person of your choosing.

If you request your credit report by mail, you should receive a copywithin three weeks. You will also receive an explanation of various codes and abbreviations.

According to the FCRA, you have the right to dispute any remark on your report that you "reasonably believe" to be inaccurate or incomplete. The act requires the credit bureau to reinvestigate those disputed items within "a reasonable period of time"—interpreted by the Federal Trade Commission as thirty days. If the bureau finds that the information was incorrect, obsolete, or could no longer be verified, it must correct or delete the information.

If the bureau does not respond to your initial dispute within a "reasonable time," follow up immediately with another letter. This time, demand that the bureau respond to your dispute immediately to prevent your being forced to take legal action. Give them about two weeks to comply and be sure to maintain copies of all correspondence.

If the bureau persists in violating your rights by refusing

to reinvestigate your legitimate dispute, send them a final letter demanding action. This time, send copies of your letter, along with the original request, to the Federal Trade Commission and your local office of the attorney general.

HOW TO DISPUTE

1. Obtain a credit report and analyze the report for items you believe to be inaccurate, incorrect, or obsolete. For example, you thought you owed $800 on your Visa card account. The account is presently under collection, but your TRW credit report shows a balance of $900. This is inaccurate, and you have a right to dispute the entire account.

2. Send the bureau a dispute form (enclosed with your credit report). If you don't have a consumer dispute form, you may copy the one at the end of this chapter or use a blank piece of paper. Question only two or three items at a time, so that your dispute will not appear to be frivolous.

A. On the dispute form, be sure to include the items you are disputing, the names of the creditors (subscribes), and the account numbers.

B. Indicate why you believe that item is being reported incorrectly. Examples: the amount owed is incorrect, the account is not yours, the account has been paid in full, the number of late payments is incorrect, etc.

3. Keep track of the date the dispute was sent. If you do not receive a response within six weeks, send a follow-up letter (see sample on page 81).

4. Obtain results of the credit bureau's reinvestigation. Most credit bureaus will notify you of the result of the investigation and send you a copy of your updated credit report.

5. Wait at least six weeks.

6. Repeat the cycle from step one for another two to three items.

7. Keep a record of all correspondence. Make copies of all credit reports, disputes, replies, and responses. If the reply is by telephone, note the date and time of call, name of the person who called, and the nature of the conversation.

THE DISPUTE CYCLE

1. Obtain credit report
2. Send dispute form
3. Credit bureau verifies
4. Disputed information checked with creditors
5. Creditors respond to credit bureau investigation
   A. Unverifiable information deleted
   B. Incorrect information corrected
   C. Correct information remains

SAMPLE REQUEST FOR CREDIT REPORT
(AFTER DENIAL)

Date

Name of Credit Bureau
Address of Credit Bureau

To Whom It May Concern:

I have been denied credit within the past thirty days based on a credit report from your company. Enclosed is a copy of the denial letter. Please send me a copy of my credit report as soon as possible.

Name
Present Address
Previous Address
Social Security Number
Date of Birth

Thank you very much for your immediate attention.

Sincerely yours,

Your Name

SAMPLE REQUEST FOR CREDIT REPORT
(NO DENIAL)

Date
Name of Credit Bureau
Address of Credit Bureau

To Whom It May Concern:

Enclosed is a check for $ _____ (amount) to cover the indicated cost of providing me with a copy of my credit report. Please send the credit report as soon as possible to the name and address below:

Name
Present Address
Previous Address
Social Security Number
Date of Birth

Thank you very much for your immediate attention.

Sincerely yours,

Your Name

SAMPLE CONSUMER DISPUTE FORM

_____ _____
Area Code Telephone No.

Personal Identification (Please Print or Type)

Name_____
      (Last)   (First) (M. Initial)   (Suffix Jr., Sr.)

Present Address _____
        (Street)   (City)   (State) (ZIP)

Former Address_____
        (Street)   (City)   (State, ZIP)

Date of Birth_____ **Social Security #** _____
      (Month/Day/Year)

I recently received a copy of the report confirming my credit history,
and I disagree with the following information:

CREDIT HISTORY

Name of Business	Account Number	Specific nature of disagreement

Public Record And Other Information

Court or Business	Case Number	Nature of disagreement

Other (i.e., information from other credit bureaus)	Item	Nature of disagreement

I understand that the information I have disputed will be rechecked when necessary at the source, and I will be notified of the results of this recheck.

_____   _____

(Signature)   (Date)

SAMPLE FOLLOW-UP LETTER TO A DISPUTE

Date

Name of Credit Bureau
Address of Credit Bureau
City, State, ZIP

Attn: Consumer Relations Department

Dear:

    On _____ (date of first dispute), I sent you a request to investigate certain items on my credit report that I believe to be incorrect or inaccurate. But as of today, six weeks have passed, and I have not yet received a response from you. Under the Fair Credit Reporting Act, you are required to respond within "a reasonable time." If the information cannot be verified, please delete it from my credit report. I would appreciate your immediate attention to this matter and your informing me of the result.

Yours sincerely,

Your Name
Address
Social Security Number
Date of Birth

SECOND FOLLOW-UP LETTER

Date

Name of Bureau
Address
City, State, ZIP

RE: Your Name
Address
Social Security Number

To Whom It May Concern:

Four weeks ago, I sent you a follow-up letter stating that you had neither responded to nor investigated my disputes of certain incorrect items found on my credit report. Copies of that letter and the original dispute letter are enclosed.

To date, you still have not complied with your obligation under the Fair Credit Reporting Act, which requires your company to ensure the correctness of reported information.

I hereby demand that you immediately remove the items disputed from my credit file based on the fact that they are either inaccurate or unverifiable. I also expect you to send me an updated copy of my credit report immediately afterward.

If I do not receive your response within the next two weeks, I will file a complaint with the Federal Trade Commission and the attorney general. In addition, I will not hesitate to retain my attorney to pursue my right to recover damages under the Fair Credit Reporting Act.

Please also forward me the names and addresses of individuals you contacted to verify the information so I may follow up. Thank you for your immediate attention to this matter.

Sincerely yours,

Your Name

CONSUMER STATEMENTS

Under the Fair Credit Reporting Act you have the right to add to your credit report a statement of up to one hundred words regarding any item(s) you wish to clarify. This statement will then appear on all subsequent reports sent to your credit grantors.

The consumer statement has often proven to be a very effective tool. It is especially useful when the amount of the particular negative account is relatively small or you have plenty of positive items to cover the single negative item.

Here are some examples of consumer statements you can use:

• "TRW, a business for profit, violates my Constitutional right to privacy by maintaining my name in its computer bank against my wishes, places me in a false light while doing so, and appropriates my name for its commercial advantage. TRW has continually and persistently violated the California Consumer Credit Agencies Act and the federal Fair Credit Reporting Act by not reporting a fair and accurate representation of my credit history. TRW does not maintain reasonable procedures to maintain maximum accuracy in the reports it keeps on me. Accordingly, this report is not accurate and should not be given such credence."

• "Attention: Due to the identification system used by TRW, it is apparent that my credit file has been merged with the file of someone else bearing the same name. Please contact either Trans Union or CBI for an accurate report."

• "Attention: Apparently someone has been using my identification to obtain credit. Please verify with me at (phone number) prior to extension of new credit."

• "Attention: This is not my account. I have never owed money to this creditor. Apparently, a mistake was made in the reporting."

• "On _____ (date), I moved to another address. I notified all creditors, including _____ (name of creditor) promptly. _____ (creditor) was slow in changing my address in its file. Subsequently, I did not receive my billing statement for _____ (how long). Once I received the statement at my new address, I paid this creditor."

• "During the period from _____ to _____, I was laid off work without advance notice. I have always paid my creditors promptly and satisfactorily before and since that period. I am now gainfully employed and have been with the same employer for _____."

Be honest yet creative in writing your consumer statement. It could be extremely effective.

CHAPTER 11

Resolving Creditor
Disputes

THIS METHOD WORKS VERY MUCH LIKE the one we discussed in the previous chapter, "Disputing with Credit Bureaus." In this case, however, the dispute letters are directed to the creditors themselves (such as department stores, collection agencies, banks, etc.) rather than the credit bureaus.

As subscribers, the creditors have direct access to your credit bureau files. They also have the authority to change or delete information from your credit report.

This method is initiated by sending the creditor a formal letter identifying the account you are disputing, stating the reason for your dispute, and demanding that it correct or delete the derogatory item. You should also inform the creditor that if the matter is not resolved quickly, you will be forced to take legal action. (See Chapter 13, "Hardball: Aggressive Legal Tactics.")

Collection agencies will sometimes refuse to change your credit rating unless specifically instructed by the creditor that assigned them the account. In one case, a credit consultant was negotiating a settlement with a collection agency on behalf of a client. The collection agency had a reputation of being a tough negotiator. After two weeks, the negotiations broke down. The consultant went directly to the bank that had assigned the account to the agency. The consultant reached a settlement with the bank, which instructed the agency to remove the account from the client's credit report.

When disputing with a creditor there are several important points to remember:

1. You must let the creditor know that it was the one at fault. For example, it provided you with substandard service, its merchandise was defective, it misplaced your check, it did not deliver the goods, or it somehow did not perform its part of the agreement.

2. You may need to send this dispute letter all the way up to the chairman of the board to get a response.

3. Even if you were at fault, you can still get positive results. For example, one woman discovered a "thirty-day late payment" on her credit report. The account was from a major department store with which she had maintained an account for more than twelve years. She was at fault for making that late payment. However, she approached the credit manager and asked him to remove the derogatory remark from her report, indicating that she had always been a good customer. The credit manager complied with her request for public-relations purposes.

The following pages contain sample letters of successful disputes with creditors. You may modify them to fit your specific situation.

SAMPLE DISPUTE LETTER TO CREDITOR

Date

Name of Creditor
Address of Creditor

      RE: _____ (Your Name)
      Address _____
      Account Number _____

To Whom It May Concern:

I have recently obtained a credit report from _____
(credit bureau). It shows that the above account with your company was
_____ days late (or that it has been charged off, or whatever reason you
are disputing). According to the best of my recollection, I have always
paid this account promptly and satisfactorily. This incorrect information
is highly injurious to my credit rating. I would appreciate it if you would
verify this information and correct it with the above-named credit
bureau immediately. If the information cannot be verified, please delete
the account from my credit report.

Please inform me as to the result of your verification as soon as possible. Your immediate attention to this matter will be greatly appreciated.

Sincerely yours,

Your Name

ALTERNATE CREDITOR DISPUTE LETTER

Date

Name of Creditor
Address of Creditor

    RE: _____ (Name)
    Address
    Account Number

To Whom It May Concern:
    I have recently obtained a credit report from _____
(credit bureau). It shows that the above account with your company was
_____ days late (or whatever dispute you are making). According to
my records, I sent payment on time for that specific incident, but your
company initially misplaced my check and later credited my account
with the correct amount. This incorrect information is highly injurious
to my credit rating. I would like you to remove this inaccurate information from my credit report immediately. If this matter is not resolved
immediately, I will be forced to bring legal action against your company
for negligence. Your immediate attention to this matter will be greatly
appreciated.

    Sincerely yours,

    Your Name

CHAPTER 12

Dynamic
Negotiation
Strategies

THE FOLLOWING STRATEGY IS THE MOST EFFECTIVE and ethical method of credit restoration. This is especially true when you consider that it is a win-win situation. The creditor gets paid, and you get the negative information removed from your credit report.

AGREEING ON A REPAYMENT RATE

Your bargaining power in this technique is your willingness to repay your creditor the money that you owe him. If the account has already been charged off or discharged in bankruptcy, your leverage will be even greater. At this point, the creditor has already accepted a loss on your account, and he does not expect to ever see or hear from you again. When he hears that you are now willing to repay the debt (or even a percentage of the debt), he'll be in a state of shock.

You should expect to repay your creditor from 70 percent to the full amount to have it remove or change the derogatory credit rating. However, if you expect to settle at 70 percent or less, you should start by offering around 40 percent.

You will also lose some of your bargaining power if the balance on the account is under $200, as the creditor may not even want to waste his time with it.

In many cases, the initial person with whom you begin negotiating does not have the authority to enter into a settlement agreement, especially since it involves changing your credit rating. Therefore, it is important that you talk directly to the supervisor or someone who is in a position to authorize the final agreement.

MAKING CREDITORS CHANGE OR DELETE INFORMATION FROM YOUR FILE

Another obstacle you may face is that many of these collection officers will tell you that it is impossible (or illegal) to change your credit rating. Therefore, it is often necessary for you to explain to them what you want and how it can be done. The creditor can use the following methods to change or delete credit information on your file:

1. All creditors who subscribe to one of the major credit bureaus use a nine-track computerized magnetic tape to report their clients' payment histories to the bureau. They send this tape to the bureau on a monthly basis. Therefore, you can request that they change the information on this tape after they receive your payment. You may also ask them to delete the account from the tape.

2. The creditor can also "bull's-eye" your account. This is an instant method of credit file correction, which is accomplished through the creditor's computer link to the credit bureau. The creditor has the capacity to pull up your account on the computer and make the necessary change automatically. By using a change of information slip, the authorized person can send the corrected information to the

data acquisition department of the credit bureau and your file will be updated.

3. The creditor can also change the information by submitting a manual update form to the consumer relations department of the credit bureau. With this method, the creditor can delete negative information but cannot change the rating from negative to positive.

When negotiating with the creditor, it is essential that you know exactly what you are trying to accomplish. Your priority is to have the account deleted or removed completely from your credit report. This is especially true when you are negotiating with a collection agency that has reported your account to the credit bureau. You definitely do not want the name of any collection agency appearing on your credit report. Their name alone is considered a negative item by most credit grantors.

POSITIVE, NONRATED, OR NEGATIVE RATING OF YOUR FILE

If the creditor will not delete the account from your report completely, your next attempt should be to have the negative remark changed to a positive remark. For example:

1. Paid Satisfactory/Paid as Agreed
2. Current Account/with No Late Payments
3. Credit Line Closed/Consumer's Request

The lowest rating you will accept in your negotiation should be "nonrated account." For example:

1. Paid
2. Settled as a Nonrated Account

Under no circumstances should you accept a negative rating, such as:

1. Paid Collection
2. Paid Charge-Off
3. Paid, Was 30 (or 60, 90, 120) Days Late

If the creditor will not delete the account or change the rating to a positive remark, then you should turn to other methods of credit restoration for that specific account.

Successful negotiation takes patience and persistence. Do not show the creditor that you are too anxious to settle. After you have made your offer, wait for the creditor to accept or make a counteroffer. Always make it clear when you begin negotiating that your only incentive to settle is to restore your credit rating. Therefore, a positive correction or deletion of the account is essential to any agreement. If a creditor is interested in settling, it knows that you will settle only if a better credit rating is part of the deal.

After reaching an agreement on the phone and before making any payment, be sure to confirm the agreement in writing by sending the creditor a settlement agreement like the one included at the end of this chapter. Have the creditor sign the agreement and return a copy to you *before* you send the money. This is essential because there have been many cases where a collection agency agreed to everything on the telephone but, after receiving the money, denied any promises had been made and refused to follow through on its end of the bargain. With a signed agreement clearly stating the responsibility of each party, both should honor their part of the contract. Otherwise, the creditor could face legal action for breach of contract as well as fraud.

Timing is essential in negotiating a good settlement agreement. A bank is a highly departmentalized institution.

When your loan is still in the current-loan servicing department, the bank has no incentive to settle with you or change your credit rating. It expects you to pay what you owe as agreed. Successful negotiating can start when the loan is in the collection department, charge-off department, or legal department. At this point, the bank has given up hope on you and should be glad to settle the account.

If you are facing a temporary cash flow problem, you can use this method to lower your monthly payments and avoid filing bankruptcy. Explain your financial problem to your creditors and offer to make monthly payments of 4 percent of the balance of the accounts. This is a reasonable offer and should be acceptable to many creditors as an alternative to bankruptcy. You can always increase your monthly payments later, when you are in a better financial position.

You may also want to consider the services of Consumer Credit Counselors, a nonprofit organization. For a nominal fee, this agency will negotiate on your behalf. You can find the address in your local telephone directory. Many lenders are more willing to work with this organization because of its national reputation.

NEGOTIATION CYCLE

1. Contact creditor by phone and reach a tentative agreement.

2. Send creditor settlement agreement requesting return of signed copy.

3. Send money order marked "Full Payment" upon receipt of signed copy.

4. Order credit report from credit bureau to ensure item is changed or deleted as agreed.

5. If credit report is unchanged, send creditor a letter demanding compliance with agreement.

SAMPLE SETTLEMENT AGREEMENT

Address

Date

Attention:
Name of Creditor
Address

RE: Account

Dear:

Confirming our previous telephone conversation on _____ _____ (date) regarding the settlement of the above account, I will pay your company $_____ as full settlement of this account. Upon receipt of the above consideration, your company has agreed to change the remark on my credit file to "Paid Satisfactorily." In addition, any references to late payment or charge-off regarding this account will be deleted from my credit file. Your cooperation in this matter is appreciated, and if this settlement agreement is acceptable to your company, please so acknowledge with your signature in the space provided below and return a copy to me. Upon receipt of this signed acknowledgment, I will immediately forward you a cashier's check in the amount stated above.

Thank you for your immediate attention and cooperation.

(Signature of authorized officer) _____
(Date) _____

Yours sincerely,

Your Name

CHAPTER 13

Hardball: Aggressive Legal Tactics

IF PREVIOUS METHODS HAVE BEEN UNSUCCESSFUL, or if a particular creditor or credit bureau persists in violating your legal rights, you may also use the court system to help restore your credit.

YOUR RIGHTS UNDER THE FAIR CREDIT REPORTING ACT

If a credit bureau refuses to investigate a legitimate dispute by claiming it is "frivolous and irrelevant," you can retain an attorney and file a lawsuit against the bureau for noncompliance with the Fair Credit Reporting Act or similar state statutes. While the trial is pending, your attorney can file a motion for injunctive relief. Since the negative remarks on your credit report may threaten your basic living—such as renting an apartment, obtaining employment, writing a check, obtaining loans for your business, etc.—the court may grant this motion.

In many cases, the matter may not be adjudicated for several years. In the meantime, your attorney can ask the court to order the credit bureau to refrain temporarily from including any derogatory items under dispute in your credit file until the case is resolved. If the court rules the motion in your favor, the credit bureau will be compelled by law to refrain from reporting the disputed derogatory information.

Another method is to file a complaint against the credit bureau in small-claims court. Terms vary among states, but in California, the filing fee is only $8, and a claimant can recover up to $200 in damages. Such damages may include denial of credit, stress, humiliation, or punitive damages for willful noncompliance with state and federal laws. If enough consumers followed this route, it would create an incentive for the credit bureaus to start obeying the law and fulfilling their responsibilities under the Fair Credit Reporting Act.

If you intend to file a lawsuit against a credit bureau, it is essential that you keep accurate records of all correspondence. You should be sure to maintain copies of credit reports, loan denials, and all other documentation relating to your case. The key to using the courts successfully is sufficient evidence.

If enough people got together, it would also be possible to file a class-action suit against a credit bureau that persists in violating the rights of consumers. This would begin with a group of individuals who have received letters from a certain credit bureau refusing to investigate their disputes. By filing a class-action suit against a major credit bureau, it would be possible to make a serious dent in the bureaucratic machinery. Class-action suits have often resulted in awards of several million dollars.

The following is a summary of your legal rights under the Fair Credit Reporting Act:

1. To be told the nature and source of the information collected about you by a credit bureau.

2. To obtain this information free of charge when you have been denied credit, insurance, or employment within thirty days. Otherwise, the reporting agency can charge a reasonable fee for the disclosure.

3. To take anyone of your choosing with you when you visit the credit bureau.

4. To be told who has received a credit report on you within the preceding six months, or within the preceding two years if the report was furnished for employment purposes.

5. To have incomplete, incorrect, or obsolete information reinvestigated and, if found to be inaccurate or unverifiable, to have such information removed from your file.

6. When a dispute between you and the credit bureau cannot be resolved, to have your version of the dispute placed in the file and included in future reports.

7. To request the credit bureau to send your consumer statement to all future credit grantors.

8. To have a credit report withheld from anyone who does not have a legitimate business need for the information.

9. To sue a company for damages if it willingly or negligently violates the law and, if the suit is successful, to collect attorney's fees and court costs.

10. To be notified if a company is requesting an investigative consumer report.

11. To request from a company that ordered an investigative report further information as to the nature and scope of the investigation.

12. To have negative information removed from your report after seven years. One major exception is bankruptcy, which may be reported for ten years.

LETTER FROM FEDERAL TRADE
COMMISSION TO AUTHOR

UNITED STATES OF AMERICA
FEDERAL TRADE COMMISSION

04/28/89

Mr. Robert Hammond:

Re: Correspondence No. 1684890011988

Dear Mr. Hammond:

Thank you for your letter concerning a problem with your credit report and a credit bureau that is reporting information about you. Enclosed for your information is a brochure describing the Fair Credit Reporting Act (FCRA) which you may find helpful.

You have the right under the FCRA to be told what information is in your file at the credit bureau and the source of the information. You can ask the credit bureau for this disclosure either in person, or by telephone if they have first sent a written request that properly identifies them (usually your name, current address, and social security number). Some credit bureaus will mail you a copy of your file, but they are not required to do so.

If you believe an item in your credit report is inaccurate or is not complete, the FCRA gives you the right to dispute this information. You should write the credit bureau and tell it that a dispute exists regarding a particular item of information. It is often useful to provide the credit bureau with any information that you might have that would assist them in their investigation efforts. We suggest that you send your dispute via certified mail, and that you retain a copy for your records.

Credit bureaus are required to investigate your dispute within a reasonable period of time, generally thirty days, unless the bureau has reasonable grounds to believe the dispute is frivolous or irrelevant. If the item is wrong or can no longer be checked, it must be dropped from your file. If, after the credit bureau has concluded its investigation, you still don't agree that your report is accurate, you should write a short statement of 100 words or less giving your side of the situation. This statement then becomes part of your credit report. At your request, the credit bureau must report the change to anyone who received a copy of your report during the past six months.

Once a credit bureau has verified an item of information, it is entitled to continue to report that information on your credit report.

If you still dispute the accuracy of the information being reported, we suggest that you contact the responsible creditor directly and attempt to resolve the problem at its source. Negative credit information generally may be reported for seven years with the exception of a bankruptcy, which may be reported for 10 years.

One important point to keep in mind is that even though you paid off a credit account that was previously delinquent, the credit bureau can still report the fact that you were behind in your payments when you finally paid the account off. A credit report showing that you paid a debt off after it became delinquent is usually considered to be adverse information by creditors, but not as adverse as a credit report showing that you haven't paid off the debt.

If you feel that your credit report does not accurately portray your creditworthiness, Regulation B—which implements the Equal Opportunity Act—provides that you have the right to present information to your prospective creditor to show that your credit report does not reflect your ability or willingness to repay. The creditor must consider this information at your request. If you know there is adverse information on your credit report, it is often best to explain the circumstances surrounding the item and to provide other positive information to the creditor at the time they complete the application.

We cannot act as your lawyer or intervene in a dispute between a consumer and a credit bureau or a reporter of information. The FCRA does give you the right to bring suit on your own behalf for willful and negligent violations of the Act. You may also be able to recover attorney's fees. If you believe the FCRA has been violated, we suggest that you consult a private attorney or your local legal services organization.

Thank you for bringing your experience to our attention.

Sincerely,

Frances Blair-Robinson
Los Angeles Regional Office
11000 Wilshire Blvd.
Federal Building
Los Angeles, CA 90024

Document(s) 5873

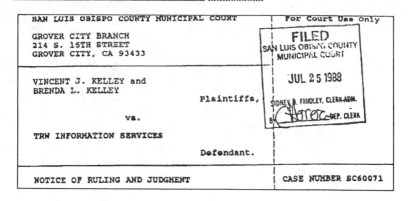

SAN LUIS OBISPO COUNTY MUNICIPAL COURT	For Court Use Only
GROVER CITY BRANCH 214 S. 15TH STREET GROVER CITY, CA 93433	**FILED** SAN LUIS OBISPO COUNTY MUNICIPAL COURT

VINCENT J. KELLEY and
BRENDA L. KELLEY
          Plaintiffs,
 	
vs.
 	
TRW INFORMATION SERVICES
          Defendant.
	JUL 25 1988
	SIDNEY D. FINDLEY, CLERK-ADM.
	BY _____ DEP. CLERK

NOTICE OF RULING AND JUDGMENT	CASE NUMBER SC60071

Based on the evidence, the Court finds for Plaintiffs and orders that judgment be entered against Defendant TRW Information Services in the amount of $500.00 plus court costs and filing fees as shown by the court records.

Although defendant is correct that the inaccuracies in defendant's credit report were not the sole reason that credit was refused on two occasions so as to entitle plaintiffs to recover the total damages claimed, those inaccuracies did cause plaintiffs to incur out-of-pocket expenses in excess of $120.00 and to experience mental suffering and stress in order to refute the misrepresentations as to their financial history and cause defendant to delete them from future reports. Defendant is engaged in the business of furnishing credit reports and charges a fee for such services. In publishing data which damages the credit standing of the persons named in the report, defendant cannot claim immunity simply because they obtain the basic data from another source. The republication of false data creates an independent grounds for liability.

DATED: July 25, 1988

HJ/md

HAROLD JOHNSON
MUNICIPAL COURT JUDGE

101

CHAPTER 14

Questions and Answers about Credit Repair

Q: IS IT REALLY POSSIBLE TO "ERASE BAD CREDIT"?

A: Yes. By following the various procedures outlined previously it is possible to remove all types of negative information from your credit files. For example, a credit bureau is required by law to reinvestigate disputed information with the creditor (subscriber). If the information is found to be inaccurate, it must be corrected. If the information is obsolete, it must be deleted. If the information can no longer be verified, it must be deleted. Also, by negotiating directly with the creditor, it is possible to have the creditor instruct the bureau to remove or correct the bad credit information in your file.

Q: What can I do with accounts that I have paid already but that show up with a negative remark?

A: Many creditors have already closed your file after you paid them off and stored the closed file at another location. They do not have the time to dig out those records and verify the information whenever someone disputes an old account. Therefore, the information may not be verified when the credit bureau reinvestigates the dispute. If the information is not verified, it must be deleted from your credit report.

Q: How do I improve my credit report after filing bankruptcy?

A: The debts that were discharged during bankruptcy will show up on your credit report as either "Charge-off" or "Bk Liq Reo." The bankruptcy itself will appear under public record information as Chapter 7 or Chapter 13. The only way to remove the bankruptcy itself from your credit report is to dispute it directly with the credit bureaus. You can usually find some mistake in the reporting of the information. Some people simply deny that they ever filed the bankruptcy, although this is definitely not recommended. Normally, the bankruptcy will remain on your credit report for up to ten years unless it is removed through dispute.

As to the items that were charged off by your creditors when you filed bankruptcy, the most effective way to remove these items is through negotiation with the creditors (see Chapter 12, "Dynamic Negotiation Strategies"). Negotiate with your creditors so that, in return for your repaying a portion of the debt, they agree to change your credit rating or delete the accounts from your credit reports.

Another alternative is to add a consumer statement to your credit report. This statement, which can be up to one hundred words, allows you to tell your side of the story. In some cases, people have indicated in their consumer statements that they never filed bankruptcy or that all the accounts included in the bankruptcy have since been paid in full.

Q: How can I remove a defaulted student loan from my credit report?

A: This will depend on who reported the account to the credit bureau. There are three possible entities: the Student

Loan Commission (i.e., the government), the bank that financed the student loan, or the collection agency. If the Student Loan Commission reported the delinquent account, the only way you can remove it is to pay off the loan in full and then dispute it with the credit bureau. You can inform the bureau that the loan has now been paid in full (only if it has, of course). The credit bureau will then have to verify the information with the Student Loan Commission. Since the commission has to service so many loans, it is very possible that it may not verify with the credit bureau that your loan was ever in default. If the bank or the collection agency reported the delinquent student-loan account, then you can use the creditor negotiation strategy outlined in Chapter 11.

Q: How do I remove a judgment from my credit report?

A: If a judgment has already been entered against you and has appeared on your credit report, there are several possible approaches you can take:

1. If you have never been served with the lawsuit, have your attorney file a "motion to vacate judgment" with the court. After the court grants you the motion (assuming the time to file such a motion has not run out), send a court-certified copy of the court decision to all the credit bureaus that have recorded your judgment and demand that they remove the judgment immediately.

2. If you have already received a judgment and you have been served, but perhaps improperly, you can still negotiate your way out of the judgment. The negotiation will involve two aspects:

A. Call the creditor and claim that you have been served improperly with the lawsuit (you can only make this claim if you did not appear for the trial and a default judgment was entered against you), but you are willing to settle the case and pay them a portion of the claim. After you come to an agreement on the amount of settlement, you will have to stipulate to the fact that the creditor has served you improperly. Next, have your attorney file a motion to vacate judgment based on defective service, with the agreement by the creditor not to go to court to contest the motion. Before the motion is filed, however, the creditor must be paid the agreed-upon settlement amount.

B. Have your attorney file the motion to vacate judgment for you. Make sure, however, that you are within the time allowed by the statute of limitation to file such a motion before you begin. After the court grants the motion, have the court clerk certify several copies of the motion and mail a copy to each of the major credit bureaus, along with a cover letter stating that you want the judgment removed from your credit reports. This is a court order, and they will have to remove the judgment from your record immediately.

3. Another alternative is to cover up your judgment with a good consumer statement. Before doing that, however, you have to satisfy the judgment and make sure the credit bureaus record the judgment as "satisfied" on your credit report. A good consumer statement should explain that you fought the lawsuit purposely for a legitimate reason, the blame is really that of the creditor who sued you, and you respect the court's final decision, having satisfied the judgment immediately.

CHAPTER 15

Starting Over with a New Credit File

WARNING: This chapter contains certain confidential information that could easily be subject to abuse or misuse. Neither the author nor publisher encourages, endorses, or recommends the use of any of these methods as a means to defraud or violate the rights of any other individual or organization. The reader is therefore encouraged to be diligent in applying this information to specific situations. Neither the author nor publisher is engaged in rendering any legal service. The services of a professional are recommended if legal advice or assistance is needed. The author and publisher hereby disclaim any personal loss or liabilities caused by the use or misuse of any information presented herein.

FILE SEGREGATION

An alternative credit file is a method of credit restoration that circumvents the credit-reporting system completely. Also referred to as "file segregation" by insiders, it is definitely the most controversial method of credit restoration. Although highly frowned upon by lenders and credit bureaus, the creation of an alternative credit file is probably the only 100-percent effective method of erasing bad credit overnight.

Several years ago a couple of Los Angeles attorneys discovered a weak link in the system of file retrieval used by the major credit bureaus. The attorneys saw that in certain cases when credit bureaus found no record for particular individuals, they would automatically create new files for them. In some cases, one person would have several files existing simultaneously, each containing different information.

FILE IDENTIFICATION SYSTEMS

After noticing that there were many more credit files than there were consumers, the attorneys realized that the weak link was in the file identification system itself. They began to develop this idea after legal research determined that the creation of such additional files did not in itself constitute an illegal act. The only exception would be if the additional credit file was used to commit fraud. The creation of a new file, however, did not in itself constitute fraud or appear to break any laws.

They decided to capitalize on this idea when they were presented with a credit file that appeared to be beyond the scope of conventional credit-restoration methods. Instead of going through the dispute process and waiting for the negative information to be deleted or negotiating with creditors, they would simply create a brand new credit file and "start over."

They began charging fees of $3,000 to $4,000 to create alternate files for their clients, or rather to advise their clients on the creation of alternate files. This information has been passed on to a select number of consultants who typically charge from $1,000 to $3,000 or more to help their clients start over with alternate files.

CIRCUMVENTION STRATEGIES

Every credit bureau has a particular system of file retrieval that allows it to identify the file of each person in that system. It is necessary to identify each file in such a manner to separate individuals with similar names and addresses. However, no bureau has yet come up with a perfect system of file identification. That is why you will often see items on your report that belong to someone else with a similar name.

In an effort to maintain maximum efficiency, the credit bureaus would prefer to set up more than one file on a single person than to risk merging several people's files into one. This is the "weak link" that allows a person to circumvent the system.

The primary variables involved in file identification are that the address and the ZIP Code run together in one file and the name and Social Security number run together as one file. To create new files, consultants have advised their clients to create a new address for themselves by using the address of a friend or relative.

In some instances, credit-repair specialists have advised their clients to change their surnames or middle initials, drop middle names, or transpose a couple of digits in their Social Security numbers.

The following strategies have proven successful in creating alternate credit files:

1. *Different last name.* Women whose last names have been changed through marriage or divorce have used this method successfully. By resorting to her maiden name, a woman may be able to circumvent the file that was created during her marriage. But she should remember not to indicate her married name on future credit applications, or the

two files will merge. A woman with a previous negative can marry a man with good credit and, by changing her name, create a new credit file overnight.

2. *Different first name and different address.* This is the most common method of alternate file creation to circumvent the identification systems of most credit bureaus. Since most people don't want to actually change their first name, it is easily accomplished by using the middle name as the first name and the first name as the middle initial. For example, if your name is John David Rockefeller, you could use David J. Rockefeller. This would not work, however, if your middle name starts with the same letter as the first letter of your first name.

It is also essential to combine the change of first name with a change of address. Do not use your present address or any of your previous addresses as your present or previous address on any future credit applications or your new file will merge with your old one.

3. *Different first name and last name.* This is accomplished by using one of the methods described in the section on changing your name.

4. *Applying for a new Social Security number with the Social Security office.* According to the Department of Health, Education, and Welfare's publication, *Records, Computers, and the Rights of Citizens*, the Social Security Act provides that "any employee may have his account number changed at any time by applying to the Social Security Board and showing good reason for the change. With that exception, only one account number will be assigned to an employee."

5. *Making up a new Social Security number.* This is a technique commonly used by individuals such as illegal aliens who do not have a legal right to work in the United States. It is important to note that each set of digits has a cer-

tain significance. The first three digits correspond to the state in which the card is requested. The second two digits represent the approximate year of issue. The final set of four digits is often used as a personal identifier.

6. *Typographical error on the credit application.* Often an individual will "accidently" transpose a couple of numbers in his Social Security number when filling out a credit application. For example, 123-45-6789 becomes 123-45-6879.

7. *Applying for a Social Security number under an alternate identity.* This is a very questionable method sometimes used by individuals who have created an alternative identity using one of the methods outlined later in this chapter.

The most comprehensive method of creating an alternative credit file will circumvent all of the major credit bureaus in the United States simultaneously. This is accomplished by using a different first or last name, a different address, and a different Social Security number. Once again, it is important to avoid using any of your previous identifying information on any future credit applications.

CHANGING YOUR NAME

1. *Use method.* This is a legal method of changing your name without a court appearance. All that you need to do is to begin using a new name of your choosing. Just start using your new name for all of your records and transactions. Obtain a new driver's license from the department of motor vehicles by simply requesting a new license and checking the box on the application that says "Name Change." This is the same method used by a woman who gets married and begins using her husband's name. The same is true when a divorced woman decides to return to the use of her maiden name. Once you have established a new name in one state, you may transfer this information to another state.

2. *Court method*. This is a more common way of establishing a new identity. You can do all the paperwork yourself or have an attorney file the required forms and accompany you to court. To determine whether you are assuming an alternative identity for fraudulent purposes, the judge will ask your reasons for changing your name. If there is no good reason why the name change should not be approved, the court will grant the name change and a copy of the declaration will be forwarded to the secretary of state.

As an adult citizen of the United States, you have the right to use any name you choose, providing that it is not used with the intent to defraud and that it does not interfere with the right of another person (such as using the name of a famous entertainer or public figure). Changing your name does not affect your legal liabilities or past debts. You are still liable for all of the past and future debts incurred under your original name. A name change does not relieve you of your responsibilities.

DECLARATION OF LEGAL NAME CHANGE

I, the undersigned, declare that the following is true and correct: (name presently using) born (name on birth certificate) in _____ County in the State of _____ on the day of _____ (month), _____ (year): _____ DO HERE-BY DECLARE my intent to change my legal name, and be henceforth exclusively known as _____ (new name).

NOTICE IS HEREBY GIVEN to all agencies of the State, all agencies of the Federal government, and creditors, and all private persons, groups, businesses, corporations, and associations of this legal change of name. I further declare that I have no intention of defrauding any person or escaping any obligation I may presently have by this act.

DATED: _____

(Old Signature) _____

(New Signature) _____

State of _____

County of _____

On _____, 19 _____, before me, _____, a notary public of the State of _____, known to me to be a person whose name is subscribed to this instrument, and acknowledged that he/she executed the same.

_____ Notary Public for Said State

_____ Date Notary Commission Expires

(Seal)

ESTABLISHING AN ALTERNATE CREDIT FILE

Once you have decided on an alternate file identification, the next step is to establish the new file in the credit-reporting system. You accomplish this by ordering a copy of your credit report using the new identifying information. You can either write to the bureaus directly or request the report through a local independent bureau.

You can also apply for credit at a department store or auto dealer using the new identifying information. If the credit report comes back as "No Record Found," a new credit file has been established.

From this point, new credit information can then be transferred or added to the newly created file.

Because of the sensitive nature of this particular technique, it is recommended that you enlist the services of a professional before proceeding. A more detailed description of the alternate credit file method, including the identification systems used by all of the major credit bureaus in the United States, is included in my previous book *Credit Secrets: How to Erase Bad Credit.*

This technique came about as a result of a need by undercover agents to establish an instant credit history when working under an assumed name.

Apply to the banks where you already have credit under your old name and ask them to issue an additional secondary card to the new name and address, with the original signor of that account as guarantor. The bank will issue that card without hesitation because the person guaranteeing the second card has a good payment history. The result is that the complete history of that credit card account, including the date the account was opened and the payment record, will appear on the new file, without any notation that it is a secondary card. This results in the addition of up to ten years of excellent credit history on your brand new credit file in a matter of weeks.

A variation of this method is to have a trusted friend or family member with good credit request an additional card to be issued in your new name. Let the person know that he or she can have the card back as soon as you receive it. You do not need to use the card itself for this technique to work. Be sure, however, that the person has an excellent payment history with this account. Otherwise, you will "inherit" a history of late payments. It may be a good idea to have your friend order a credit report first to make certain that the account has been reported accurately. By requesting several additional cards to be issued, it is possible to establish AAA-1 credit in less than thirty days.

Enclosed is a sample request letter for an additional credit card. After you have sent this letter, you will receive either a secondary credit card or a credit application for a secondary credit card. If you receive an application for a secondary card, your friend will fill out the applicant information and you will complete the information under the coapplicant category. Send in the application and wait for your new card.

After you have received your secondary cards, wait a few weeks and then order your credit reports from each of the major credit bureaus. Your reports should now reflect the credit histories of the additional accounts. This process can be repeated with several major credit cards and department store cards, and the credit history established by the primary cardholder will appear on your new credit file.

This technique can also be used when your friend or family member applies for a new credit card. All you need to do is to have him or her add your name as an additional cardholder (not coapplicant) to the application.

NOTE: The methods outlined in this chapter are

completely legal—as long as there is no intention to defraud and no one else's rights are violated.

Creating a new credit file does not relieve you of your previous debts or responsibilities. Once you have established credit under an alternate file, be diligent in using your new financial standing wisely and taking care of your obligations in an ethical manner.

SAMPLE REQUEST LETTER FOR
SECONDARY CREDIT CARD

Date

Name of Bank/Department Store
Credit Card Department
Address

> RE: Name of Primary Cardholder
> Address of Primary Cardholder
> Account Number (of Credit Card)

To Whom It May Concern:

As the above-named credit cardholder, I would like to request that a secondary card be issued to the following person, and I will guarantee the payment on this account:

Name: Secondary Card Applicant
Address: Secondary Applicant
Social Security Number: Secondary Applicant
Date of Birth: Secondary Applicant

Your cooperation and immediate attention to this matter will be greatly appreciated.

Sincerely yours,

Signature of Primary Cardholder

PART THREE

Appendices

APPENDIX A

The Fair Credit Reporting Act

THE FAIR CREDIT REPORTING ACT is the law that governs credit bureaus. TRW played a significant role in authoring the act. Although the entire act is contained within this book, you should at least be familiar with three main sections:

Section 604

Permissible purposes for reports. This section outlines under what circumstances a report may be pulled.

Section 605

Obsolete information. This section requires that the credit bureau purge its files of adverse credit information within seven years from the date of occurrence. An exception to this rule is bankruptcy information, which may be reported for ten years.

Section 611

Procedure in case of disputed accuracy. Section 611 is a self-help mechanism designed to correct errors and misleading information from the credit file.

SECTIONS:

601. Short Title

602. Findings and Purpose

603. Definitions and Rules of Construction

604. Permissible Purposes of Reports

605. Obsolete Information

606. Disclosure of Investigative Consumer Reports

607. Compliance Procedures

608. Disclosures of Governmental Agencies

609. Disclosure to Consumers

610. Conditions of Disclosure to Consumers

611. Procedure in Case of Disputed Accuracy

612. Charges for Certain Disclosures

613. Public Record Information for Employment Purposes

614. Restrictions on Investigative Consumer Reports

615. Requirements on Users of Consumer Reports

616. Civil Liability for Willful Noncompliance

617. Civil Liability for Negligent Noncompliance

618. Jurisdiction of Courts; Limitation of Actions

619. Obtaining Information under False Pretenses

620. Unauthorized Disclosures by Officers or Employees

621. Administrative Enforcement

622. Relation to State Laws

Section 601

The Consumer Credit Protection Act is amended by adding at the end thereof the following new title:

TITLE VI —
CONSUMER CREDIT REPORTING

Short Title

This title may be cited as the Fair Credit Reporting Act.

Section 602 Findings and Purpose

(a) The Congress makes the following findings:

(1) The banking system is dependent upon fair and accurate credit reporting. Inaccurate credit reports directly impair the efficiency of the banking system, and unfair credit reporting methods undermine the public confidence which is essential to the continued functioning of the banking system.

(2) An elaborate mechanism has been developed for investigating and evaluating the credit worthiness, credit standing, credit capacity, character, and general reputation of consumers.

(3) Consumer reporting agencies have assumed a vital role in assembling and evaluating consumer credit and other information on consumers.

(4) There is a need to insure that consumer reporting

agencies exercise their grave responsibilities with fairness, impartiality, and a respect for the consumer's right to privacy.

(b) It is the purpose of this title to require that consumer reporting agencies adopt reasonable procedures for meeting the needs of commerce for consumer credit, personnel, insurance, and other information in a manner which is fair and equitable to the consumer with regard to the confidentiality, accuracy, relevancy, and proper utilization of such information in accordance with the requirements of this title.

Section 603 Definitions and Rules of Construction

(a) Definitions and rules of construction set forth in this section are applicable for the purposes of this title.

(b) The term "person" means any individual, partnership, corporation, trust, estate, cooperative, association, government or governmental subdivision or agency, or other entity.

(c) The term "consumer" means an individual.

(d) The term "consumer report" means any written, oral, or other communication of any information by a consumer reporting agency bearing on a consumer's creditworthiness, credit standing, credit capacity, character, general reputation, personal characteristics, or mode of living which is used or expected to be used or collected in whole or in part for the purpose of serving as a factor in establishing the consumer's eligibility for

(1) credit or insurance to be used primarily for personal, family, or household purposes, or

(2) employment purposes, or

(3) other purposes authorized under section 604. The term does not include:

(A) any report containing information solely as to transactions or experiences between the consumer and the person making the report;

(B) any authorization or approval of a specific extension of credit directly or indirectly by the issuer of a credit card or similar device; or

(C) any report in which a person who has been requested by a third party to make a specific extension of credit directly or indirectly to a consumer conveys his decision with respect to such request, if the third party advises the consumer of the name and address of the person to whom the request was made and such person makes the disclosures to the consumer required under section 615.

(e) The term "investigative consumer report" means a consumer report or portion thereof in which information on a consumer's character, general reputation, personal characteristics, or mode of living is obtained through personal interviews with neighbors, friends, or associates of the consumer reported on or with others with whom he is acquainted or who may have knowledge concerning any such items of information. However, such information shall not include specific factual information on a consumer's credit record obtained directly from a creditor of the consumer or from a consumer reporting agency when such information was obtained directly from a creditor of the consumer or from the consumer.

(f) The term "consumer reporting agency" means any person which, for monetary fees, dues, or on a cooperative nonprofit basis, regularly engages in whole or in part in the practice of assembling or evaluating consumer credit information or other information on consumers for the purpose of furnishing consumer reports to third parties, and which uses any means or facility or interstate commerce for the purpose of preparing or furnishing consumer reports.

(g) The term "file" when used in connection with information on any consumer, means all of the information on that consumer recorded and retained by a consumer reporting agency regardless of how the information is stored.

(h) The term "medical information" means information or records obtained with the consent of the individual to whom it relates, from licensed physicians or medical practitioners, hospitals, clinics, or other medical or medically related facilities.

Section 604 Permissible Purpose of Reports

A consumer reporting agency may furnish a consumer report under the following circumstances and no other:

(1) In response to the order of a court having jurisdiction to issue such an order.

(2) In accordance with the written instructions of the consumer to whom it relates.

(3) To a person which it has reason to believe —

(A) intends to use the information in connection with a credit transaction involving the consumer on whom the information is to be furnished and involving the extension of credit to, or review or collection of an account of, the consumer, or

(B) intends to use the information for employment purposes; or

(C) intends to use the information in connection with the underwriting of insurance involving the consumer; or

(D) intends to use the information in connection with a determination of the consumer's eligibility for a license or other benefit granted by a governmental instrumentality required by law to consider an applicant's financial responsibility or status; or

(E) otherwise has a legitimate business need for the information in connection with a business transaction involving the consumer.

Section 605 Obsolete Information

(a) Except as authorized under subsection (b), no

consumer reporting agency may make any consumer report containing any of the following items of information:

(1) Cases under title 11 of the United States Code or under the Bankruptcy Act that, from the date of entry of the order for relief or the date of adjudication, as the case may be, antedate the report by more than 10 years.

(2) Suits and judgments which, from date of entry, antedate the report by more than seven years or until the governing statute of limitations has expired, whichever is the longer period.

(3) Paid tax liens which, from date of payment, antedate the report by more than seven years.

(4) Accounts placed for collection or charged to profit and loss which antedate the report by more than seven years.

(5) Records of arrest, indictment, or conviction of crime which, from date of disposition, release, or parole, antedate the report by more then seven years.

(6) Any other adverse item of information which antedates the report by more than seven years.

(b) The provisions of subsection (a) are not applicable in the case of any consumer credit report to be used in connection with:

(1) a credit transaction involving, or which may

reasonably be expected to involve, a principal amount of $50,000 or more;

(2) the underwriting of life insurance involving, or which may reasonably be expected to involve, a face amount of $50,000 or more; or

(3) the employment of any individual at an annual salary which equals, or which may reasonably be expected to equal $20,000, or more.

Section 606 Disclosure of Investigative Consumer Reports

(a) A person may not procure or cause to be prepared an investigative consumer report on any consumer unless —

(1) It is clearly and accurately disclosed to the consumer that an investigative consumer report including information as to his character, general reputation, personal characteristics, and mode of living, whichever are applicable, may be made, and such disclosure —

(A) is made in a writing mailed, or otherwise delivered, to the consumer, not later than three days after the date on which the report was first requested, and

(B) includes a statement informing the consumer of his right to request the additional disclosures provided for under subsection (b) of this section; or

(2) the report is to be used for employment purposes for which the consumer has not specifically applied.

(b) Any person who procures or causes to be prepared an investigative consumer report on any consumer shall, upon written request made by the consumer within a reasonable period of time after receipt by him of the disclosure required by subsection (a) (1), shall make a complete and accurate disclosure of the nature and scope of the investigation requested. This disclosure shall be made in a writing mailed, or otherwise delivered, to the consumer not later than five days after the date on which the request for such disclosure was received from the consumer or such report was first requested, whichever is the later.

(c) No person may be held liable for any violation of subsection (a) or (b) of this section if he shows by a preponderance of the evidence that at the time of the violation he maintained reasonable procedures to assure compliance with subsection (a) or (b).

Section 607 Compliance Procedures

(a) Every consumer reporting agency shall maintain reasonable procedures designed to avoid violations of section 605 and to limit the furnishing of consumer reports to the purposes listed under section 604. These procedures shall require that prospective users of the information identify themselves, certify the purposes for which the information is sought, and certify that the information will be used for no other purpose. Every consumer reporting agency shall make a reasonable effort to verify the identity of a new prospective user and the uses certified by such prospective user prior to furnishing such prospective user a consumer report. No consumer reporting agency may furnish a consumer report to any person if it has reasonable grounds for believing that the consumer report will not be used for a purpose listed in section 604.

(b) Whenever a consumer reporting agency prepares a consumer report it shall follow reasonable procedures to assure maximum possible accuracy of the information concerning the individual about whom the report relates.

Section 608 Disclosures to Governmental Agencies

Notwithstanding the provisions of section 604, a consumer reporting agency may furnish identifying information respecting any consumer, limited to his name, address, former addresses, places of employment, or former places of employment, to a governmental agency.

Section 609 Disclosures to Consumers

(a) Every consumer reporting agency shall upon requested and proper identification of any consumer, clearly and accurately disclose to the consumer:

(1) The nature and substance of all information (except medical information) in its files on the consumer at the time of the request.

(2) The sources of the information; except that the sources of information acquired solely for use in preparing an investigative consumer report and actually used for no other purpose need not be disclosed: Provided, that in the event an action is brought under this title, such sources shall be available to the plaintiff under appropriate discovery procedures in the court in which the action is brought.

(3) The recipients of any consumer report on the consumer which it has furnished —

(A) for employment purposes within the two-year period preceding the request, and

(B) for any other purpose within the six-month period preceding the request.

(b) the requirements of subsection (a) respecting the disclosure of sources of information and the recipients of consumer reports do not apply to information received or consumer reports furnished prior to the effective date of this title except to the extent that the matter involved is contained in the files of the consumer reporting agency on that date.

Section 610 Conditions of Disclosure to Consumers

(a) A consumer reporting agency shall make the disclosures required under section 609 during normal business hours and on reasonable notice.

(b) The disclosures required under section 609 shall be made to the consumer —

(1) in person if he appears in person and furnishes proper identification; or

(2) by telephone if he has made a written request, with proper identification, for telephone disclosure and the toll charge, if any, for the telephone call is prepared by or charged directly to the consumer.

(c) Any consumer reporting agency shall provide trained personnel to explain to the consumer any information furnished to him pursuant to section 609.

(d) The consumer shall be permitted to be accompanied by one other person of his choosing, who shall furnish reasonable identification. A consumer reporting agency may require the consumer to furnish a written statement granting permission to the consumer reporting agency to discuss the consumer's file in such person's presence.

(e) Except as provided in sections 616 and 617, no consumer may bring any action or proceeding in the nature of defamation, invasion of privacy, or negligence with respect to the reporting of information against any consumer reporting agency, any user of information, or any person who furnishes information to a consumer reporting agency, based on information disclosed pursuant to section 609, 610, or 615, except as to false information furnished with malice or willful intent to injure such consumer.

Section 611 Procedure in Case of Disputed Accuracy

(a) If the completeness or accuracy of any item of information contained in his file is disputed by a consumer, and such dispute is directly conveyed to the consumer reporting agency by the consumer, the consumer reporting agency shall within a reasonable period of time reinvestigate and record the current status of that information unless it has reasonable grounds to believe that the dispute by the consumer is frivolous or irrelevant. If after such reinvestigation such information is found to be inaccurate or can no longer be verified, the consumer reporting agency shall promptly delete such information. The presence of contradictory information in the consumer's file does not in and of itself constitute reasonable grounds for believing the dispute is frivolous or irrelevant.

(b) If the reinvestigation does not resolve the dispute, the consumer may file a brief statement setting forth the nature of the dispute. The consumer reporting agency may limit such statements to not more than one hundred words if it provides the consumer with assistance in writing a clear summary of the dispute.

(c) Whenever a statement of a dispute is filed, unless there is reasonable grounds to believe that it is frivolous or irrelevant, the consumer reporting agency shall, in any subsequent consumer report containing the information in question, clearly note that it is disputed by the consumer and provide either the consumer's statement or a clear and accurate codification or summary thereof.

(d) Following any deletion of information which is found to be inaccurate or whose accuracy can no longer be verified or any notation as to disputed information, the consumer reporting agency shall, at the request of the consumer, furnish notification that the item has been deleted or the statement, codification or summary pursuant to subsection (b) or (c) to any person specifically designated by the consumer who has within two years prior thereto received a consumer report for employment purposes, or within six months prior thereto received a consumer report for any other purpose, which contained the deleted or disputed information. The consumer reporting agency shall clearly and conspicuously disclose to the consumer his rights to make such a request. Such disclosure shall be made at or prior to the time the information is deleted or the consumer's statement regarding the disputed information is received.

Section 612 Charges for Certain Disclosures

A consumer reporting agency shall make all disclosures pursuant to section 609 and furnish all consumer reports pursuant to section 611 (d) without charge to the consumer if, within thirty days after receipt by such consumer of a notification pursuant to section 615 or notification from a debt collection agency affiliated with such consumer reporting agency stating that the consumer's credit rating may be or has been adversely affected, the consumer makes a request under section 609 or 611 (d).

Otherwise, the consumer reporting agency may impose a reasonable charge on the consumer for making disclosure to such consumer pursuant to section 609, the charge for which shall be indicated to the consumer prior to making disclosure; and for furnishing notifications, statements, summaries, or codifications to person designated by the consumer pursuant to section 611 (d), the charge for which shall be indicated to the consumer prior to furnishing such information and shall not exceed the charge that the consumer reporting agency would impose on each designated recipient for a consumer report except that no charge may be made for notifying such persons of the deletion of information which is found to be inaccurate or which can no longer be verified.

Section 613 Public Record Information for Employment Purposes

A consumer reporting agency which furnishes a consumer report for employment purposes and which for that purpose compiles and reports items of information on consumers which are matters of public record and are likely to have an adverse effect upon a consumer's ability to obtain employment shall —

(1) at the time such public record information is reported to the use of such consumer report, notify the consumer of the fact that public record information is being reported by the consumer reporting agency, together with the name and address of the person to whom such information is being reported; or

(2) maintain strict procedures designed to insure that whenever public record information which is likely to have an adverse effect on a consumer's ability to obtain employment is reported it is complete and up

137

to date. For purposes of this paragraph, items of public record relating to arrests, indictments, convictions, suits, tax liens, and outstanding judgments shall be considered up to date if the current public record status of the item at the time of the report is reported.

Section 614 Restrictions on Investigative Consumer Reports

Whenever a consumer reporting agency prepares an investigative consumer report, no adverse information in the consumer report (other than information which is a matter of public record) may be included in a subsequent consumer report unless such adverse information has been verified in the process of making such subsequent consumer report, or the adverse information was received within the three-month period preceding the date the subsequent report is furnished.

Section 615 Requirements on Users of Consumer Reports

(a) Whenever credit or insurance for personal, family, or household purposes, or employment involving a consumer is denied or the charge for such credit or insurance is increased either wholly or partly because of information contained in a consumer report from a consumer reporting agency, the user of the consumer report shall so advise the consumer against whom such adverse action has been taken and supply the name and address of the consumer reporting agency making the report.

(b) Whenever credit for personal, family, or household purposes involving a consumer is denied or the charge for such credit is increased either wholly or partly because of information obtained from a person other than a consumer reporting agency bearing upon the consumer's creditworthiness, credit standing, credit capacity, character, general reputation, personal characteristics, or mode of living, the user of such information shall, within a reasonable period of time, upon the consumer's written request for the reasons for such adverse action received within sixty days after learning of such adverse action, disclose the nature of the information to the consumer. The user of such information shall clearly and accurately disclose to the consumer his right to make such written request at the time such adverse action is communicated to the consumer.

(c) No person shall be held liable for any violation of this section if he can show by a preponderance of the evidence that at the time of the alleged violation he maintained reasonable procedures to assure compliance with the provisions of subsections (a) and (b).

Section 616 Civil Liability for Willful Noncompliance

Any consumer reporting agency or user of information which willfully fails to comply with any requirement imposed under this title with respect to any consumer is liable to the consumer in an amount equal to the sum of —

(1) any actual damages sustained by the consumer as a result of the failure;

(2) such amount of punitive damages as the court may allow; and

(3) in the case of any successful action to enforce any liability under this section, the costs of the action together with reasonable attorney's fees as determined by the court.

Section 617 Civil Liability for Negligent Noncompliance

Any consumer reporting agency or user of information which is negligent in failing to comply with any requirement imposed under this title with respect to any consumer is liable to that consumer in an amount equal to the sum of —

(1) any actual damages sustained by the consumer as a result of the failure;

(2) in the case of any successful action to enforce any liability under this section, the costs of the action together with reasonable attorney's fees as determined by the court.

Section 618 Jurisdiction of Courts; Limitations of Actions

An action to enforce any liability created under this title may be brought in any appropriate United States District Court without regard to the amount in controversy, or in any other court of competent jurisdiction, within two years from the date on which the liability arises, except that where a defendant has materially and willfully misrepresented any information required under this title to be disclosed to an individual and the information so misrepresented is material to the establishment of the defendant's liability to that individual under this title, the action may be brought at any time within two years after discovery by the individual of the misrepresentation.

Section 619 Obtaining Information under False Pretenses

Any person who knowingly and willfully obtains information on a consumer from a consumer reporting agency under false pretenses shall be fined not more that $5,000, or imprisoned not more than one year, or both.

Section 620 Unauthorized Disclosures by Officers or Employees

Any officer or employee of a consumer reporting agency who knowingly and willfully provides information concerning an individual from the agency's files to a person not authorized to receive that information shall be fined not more than $5,000, or imprisoned not more than one year, or both.

Section 621 Administrative Enforcement

(a) Compliance with the requirements imposed under this title shall be enforced under the Federal Trade Commission Act by the Federal Trade Commission with respect to consumer reporting agencies and all other persons subject thereto, except to the extent that enforcement of the requirements imposed under this title is specifically committed to some other government agency under subsection (b) hereof. For the purpose of the exercise by the Federal Trade Commission of its functions and posers under the Federal Trade Commission Act, a violation of any requirement or prohibition imposed under this title shall constitute an unfair or deceptive act or practice in commerce in violation of section 5 (a) of the Federal Trade Commission Act and shall be subject to enforcement by the Federal Trade Commission under section 5 (b) thereof with respect to any consumer reporting agency or person subject to enforcement by the Federal Trade Commission pursuant to this subsection, irrespective of whether that person is engaged in commerce or meets any other jurisdictional tests in the Federal Trade Commission Act. The Federal Trade Commission shall have such procedural, investigative, and enforcement powers, including the power to issue procedural rules in enforcing compliance with the requirements imposed under this title and to require the filing of reports, the production of documents, and the appearance of witnesses as though the applicable terms and conditions of the Federal Trade Commission Act were part of this title. Any person violating any of the provisions of this title shall be subject to the penalties and entitled to the privileges and immunities provided in the Federal Trade Commission Act as though the applicable terms and provisions thereof were part of this title.

(b) Compliance with the requirements imposed under this title with respect to consumer reporting agencies and persons who use consumer reports from such agencies shall be enforced under —

(1) section 8 of the Federal Deposit Insurance Act, in the case of:

(A) national banks, by the Comptroller of the Currency;

(B) member banks of the Federal Reserve System (other than national banks), by the Federal Reserve Board; and

(C) banks insured by the Federal Deposit Insurance Corporation (other than members of the Federal Reserve System), by the Board of Directors of the Federal Deposit Insurance Corporation.

(2) section 5 (d) of the Home Owners Loan Act of 1933, section 407 of the National Housing Act, and sections 6 (i) and 17 of the Federal Home Loan Bank Act by the Federal Home Loan Bank Board (acting directly or through the Federal Savings and Loan Insurance Corporation), in the case of any institution subject to any of those provisions;

(3) the Federal Credit Union Act, by the Administrator of the National Credit Union Administration with respect to any federal Credit Union;

(4) the Acts to regulate commerce, by the Interstate Commerce Commission with respect to any common carrier subject to those Acts;

(5) the Federal Aviation Act of 1958, by the Civil Aeronautics Board with respect to any air carrier or foreign air carrier subject to that Act; and

(6) the Packers and Stockyards Act, 1921 (except as provided in section 406 of that Act), by the Secretary of Agriculture with respect to any activities subject to that Act.

(c) For the purpose of the exercise by any agency referred to in subsection (b) of its powers under any Act referred to in that subsection, a violation of a requirement imposed under this title shall be deemed to be a violation of a requirement imposed under the Act. In addition to its powers under any provision of law specifically referred to in subsection (b), each of the agencies referred to in that subsection may exercise for the purpose of enforcing compliance with any requirement imposed under this title and other authority conferred on it by law.

Section 622 Relation to State Laws

This title does not annul, alter, affect, or exempt any person subject to the provisions of this title from complying with the laws of any State with respect to the collection, distribution, or use of any information on consumers, except to the extent that those laws are inconsistent with any provision of this title, and then only to the extent of the inconsistency.

144

APPENDIX B

*Equal Credit
Opportunity Act
15 U.S.C. 1691–1691c*

701 Prohibited Discrimination: Reasons for Adverse Action.

(a) It shall be unlawful for any creditor to discriminate against any applicant, with respect to any aspect of a credit transaction —

(1) on the basis of race, color, religion, national origin, sex or marital status, or age (provided the applicant has the capacity to contract):

(2) because all or part of the applicant's income derives from any public assistance program; or

(3) because the applicant has in good faith exercised any right under the Consumer Credit Protection Act.

(b) It shall not constitute discrimination for purposes of this title for a creditor —

(1) to make an inquiry of martial status if such inquiry is for the purpose of ascertaining the creditor rights and remedies applicable to the particular extension of credit and not to discriminate in a determination of creditworthiness;

(2) to make an inquiry of the applicant's age or whether the applicant's income derives from any public assistance program if such inquiry is for the purpose of determining the amount and probable continuance of income levels, credit history, or other pertinent element of creditworthiness as provided in regulations of the Board:

(3) to use any empirically derived credit system which considers age if such system is demonstrably and statistically sound in accordance with regulations of the Board, except that in the operation of such system the age of an elderly applicant may not be assigned a negative factor or value; or

(4) to make an inquiry or to consider the age of an elderly applicant when the age of such applicant is to be used by the creditor in the extension of credit in favor of such applicant.

(c) It is not a violation of this section for a creditor to refuse to extend credit offered pursuant to —

(1) any credit assistance program expressly authorized by law for an economically disadvantaged class of persons;

(2) any credit assistance program administered by a nonprofit organization for its members or an economically disadvantaged class of persons; or

(3) any special purpose credit program offered by a profit-making organization to meet special social needs, which meets standards prescribed in regulations by the Board; if such refusal is required by or made pursuant to such program.

(d)

(1) Within thirty days (or such longer reasonable time as specified in regulations of the Board for any class of credit transaction) after receipt of a completed application for credit, a creditor shall notify the applicant of its action on the application.

(2) Each applicant against whom adverse action is taken shall be entitled to a statement of reasons for such action from the creditor. A creditor satisfies this obligation by —

(A) providing statements of reasons in writing as a matter of course to applicants against whom adverse action is taken; or

(B) giving written notification of adverse action which discloses (i) the applicant's right to a statement of reasons within thirty days after receipt by the creditor of a request made within sixty days after such notification, and (ii) the identity of the person or office from which such statement may be obtained. Such statement may be given orally if the written notification advises the applicant of his right to have the statement of reasons confirmed in writing on written request.

(3) A statement of reasons meets the requirements of this section only if it contains the specific reasons for the adverse action taken.

(4) Where a creditor has been requested by a third party to make a specific extension of credit directly or indirectly to an applicant, the notification and statement of reasons required by this subsection may be made directly by such creditor, or indirectly through the third party, provided in either case that the identity of the creditor is disclosed.

(5) The requirements of paragraph (2), (3), or (4) may be satisfied by verbal statements or notification in the case of any creditor who did not act on more than 150 applications during the calendar year preceding the calendar year in which the adverse action is taken, as determined under regulations of the Board.

(6) For purposes of this subsection, the term "adverse action" means a denial or revocation of credit, a change in the terms of an existing credit arrangement, or a refusal to grant credit in substantially the amount or on substantially the terms requested. Such term does not include a refusal to extend additional credit under an existing credit arrangement where the applicant is delinquent or otherwise in default, or where such additional credit would exceed a previously established credit limit. (Amended by Act of 3/23/76, P.L. 94-239, eff. 3/23/77.)

702 *Definitions*

(a) The definition and rules of construction set forth

148

in the section are applicable for the purpose of this title.

(b) The term "applicant" means any person who applies to a creditor directly for an extension, renewal, or continuation of credit, or applies to a creditor, indirectly by use of an existing credit plan for an amount exceeding a previously established credit limit.

(c) The term "Board" refers to the Board of Governors of the Federal Reserve System.

(d) The term "credit" means the right granted by a creditor to a debtor to defer payment of debt or to incur debts and defer its payment or to purchase property or services and defer payment therefore.

(e) The term "creditor" means any person who regularly extends, renews, or continues credit; any person who regularly arranges for the extension, renewal, or continuation of credit; or any assignee of an original creditor who participates in the decision to extend, renew, or continue credit.

(f) The term "person" means a natural person, a corporation, government or governmental subdivision or agency, trust, estate, partnership, cooperative, or association.

(g) Any reference to any requirement imposed under this title or any provision thereof includes reference to the regulations of the Board under this title or the provision thereof in question.

703 Regulations

(a) The Board shall prescribe regulations to carry out the purposes of this title. These regulations may contain but are not limited to such classifications, differentiations, or other provision, and may provide for such adjustments and exceptions for any class of transactions, as in the judgment of the Board are necessary or proper to effectuate the purposes of this title, to prevent circumvention or evasion thereof, or to facilitate or substantiate compliance therewith. Such regulations shall be prescribed as soon as possible after the date of enactment of this Act, but in no event later than the effective date of this Act. In particular, such regulations may exempt from one or more of the provisions of this title any class of transactions not primarily for personal, family, or household purposes, if the Board makes an express finding that the application of such provision or provisions would not contribute substantially to carrying out the purposes of this title.

(b) The Board shall establish a Consumer Advisory Council to advise and consult with it in the exercise of its functions under the Consumer Credit Protection Act and to advise and consult with it in the exercise of its functions under the Consumer Credit Protection Act and to advise and consult with it concerning other consumer related matters it may place before the council. In appointing the members of the Council, the Board shall seek to achieve a fair representation of the interests of creditors and consumers. The Council shall meet from time to time at the call of the Board. Members of the Council who are not regular full-time employees of the United States shall, while attending meetings of such Council, be entitled to receive compensation at a rate fixed by the Board, but not exceeding $100 per day, including travel time. Such members may be allowed travel expenses, including transportation and subsistence, while away from their homes or regular place of business. (Amended by Act of 3-23-76, P.L. 94-239 eff. 3-23-76.)

704 Administrative Enforcement

(a) Compliance with the requirements imposed under this title shall be enforced under:

(1) Section 8 of the Federal Deposit Insurance Act, in the case of —

(A) national banks, by the Comptroller of the Currency,

(B) member banks of the Federal Reserve System (other than national banks), by the Board,

(C) banks insured by the Federal Deposit Insurance Corporation (other than members of the Federal Reserve System), by the Board of Directors of the Federal Deposit Insurance Corporation.

(2) Section 5(d) of the Home Owners Loan Act of 1933, section 407 of the National Housing Act, and sections 6(i) and 17 of the Federal Home Loan Bank Act, by the Federal Home Loan Bank Board (acting directly or through the Federal Savings and Loan

Insurance Corporation), in the case of any institution subject to any of those provisions.

(3) The Federal Credit Union Act, by the Administrator of the National Credit Union Administration with respect to any Federal Credit Union.

(4) The Acts to regulate commerce by the Interstate Commerce Commission with respect to any common carrier subject to those Acts.

(5) The Federal Aviation Act of 1958, by the Civil Aeronautics Board with respect to any air carrier or foreign air carrier subject to that Act.

(6) The Packers and Stockyards Act of 1921 (except as provided in section 406 of the Act), by the Secretary of Agriculture with respect to any activities subject to that act.

(7) The Farm Credit Act of 1971, by the Farm Credit Administration with respect to any Federal land bank, Federal land bank association, Federal intermediate credit bank, and production credit association;

(8) The Securities Exchange Act of 1934, by the Securities and Exchange Commission with respect to brokers and dealers; and

(9) The Small Business Investment Act of 1958, by the Small Business Administration, with respect to small business investment companies.

(b) For the purpose of the exercise by an agency referred to in subsection (a) of its power under any Act referred to in that subsection, a violation of any requirement imposed under this title shall be deemed to be a violation of a requirement imposed under that Act. In addition to its powers under any provision of law specifically referred to in subsection (a), each of the agencies referred to in that subsection may exercise for the purpose of enforcing compliance with any requirement imposed under this title, any other authority conferred on it by law. The exercise of the authorities of any of the agencies referred to in subsection (a) for the purpose of enforcing compliance with any requirement imposed under this title shall in no way preclude the exercise of such authorities for the purpose of enforcing compliance with any other provision of law not relating to the prohibition of discrimination on the basis of sex or marital status with respect to any aspect of a credit transaction.

705 Relation to State Laws

(a) A request for the signature of both parties to a marriage for the purpose of creating a valid lien, passing clear title, waiving inchoate rights to a property, or assigning earnings, shall not constitute discrimination under this title: Provided, however, That this provision shall not be construed to permit a creditor to take sex or martial status into account in connection with the evaluation of creditworthiness of any applicant.

(b) Consideration or application of State property

laws directly or indirectly affecting creditworthiness shall not constitute discrimination for purposes of this title.

(c) Any provision of State law which prohibits the separate extension of consumer credit to each party to a marriage shall not apply in any case where each party to a marriage voluntarily applies for a separate credit from the same creditor: Provided, that in any case where such a State law is so preempted, each party to the marriage shall be solely responsible for the debt so contracted.

(d) When each party to a marriage separately and voluntarily applies for and obtains separate credit accounts with the same creditor, those accounts shall not be aggregated or otherwise combined for purposes of determining permissible finance charges or permissible loan ceilings under the laws of any State or of the United States.

(e) Where the same act or omission constitutes a violation of this title and of applicable State law, a person aggrieved by such State law, but not both. This election of remedies shall not apply to court actions in which the relief sought does not include monetary damages or to administrative actions.

(f) This title does not annul, alter or affect, or exempt any person subject to the provisions of this title from complying with the laws of any State with respect to credit discrimination, except to the extent that those laws are inconsistent with any provision of this title, and then only to the extent of the inconsistency. The

154

Board is authorized to determine whether such inconsistencies exist. The Board may not determine that any State law is inconsistent with any provision of this title if the Board determines that such law gives greater protection to the applicant.

(g) The Board shall be regulation exempt from the requirements of sections 701 and 702 of this title any class of credit transactions within any State if it determines that under the law of that State that class of transactions is subject to requirements substantially similar to those imposed under this title or that such law gives greater protection to the applicant and that there is adequate provision for enforcement. Failure to comply with any requirement of such State law in any transaction so exempted shall constitute a violation of this title for the purposes of section 706. (Amended by Act of 3 -23-76, P.L. 94-239, eff. 3-23-76.)

706 Civil Liability

(a) Any creditor who fails to comply with any requirement imposed under this title shall be liable to the aggrieved applicant for any actual damages sustained by such applicant acting either in an individual capacity or as a member of a class.

(b) Any creditor, other than a government of governmental subdivision or agency, who fails to comply with any requirement imposed under this title shall be liable to the aggrieved applicant for punitive damages in an amount not greater than $10,000, in addition to any actual damages provided in subsection (a), except that in the case of a class action the total recovery under this subsection shall not exceed the lesser or $500,000 or 1 per centum of the net worth of the creditor. In determining the amount of such damages in any action, the court shall consider, among other relevant factors, the amount of any actual damages awarded, the frequency and persistence of failures of compliance by the creditor, the resources of the creditor, the number of persons adversely affected, and the extent to which the creditor's failure of compliance was intentional.

(c) Upon application by an aggrieved applicant, the appropriate United States district court or any other court of competent jurisdiction may grant such equitable and declaratory relief as is necessary to enforce the requirements imposed under this title.

(d) In the case of any successful action under subsection (a), (b), or (c), the costs of the action, together with a reasonable attorney's fee as determined by the court, shall be added to any damages awarded by the court under such subsection.

(e) No provision of this title imposing liability shall apply to any act done or omitted in good faith in conformity with any official rule, regulation, or interpretation thereof by the Board or in conformity with any interpretation or approval by an official or employee of the Federal Reserve System duly authorized by the Board to issue such interpretations or approvals under such procedures as the Board may prescribe therefore, notwithstanding that after such act or omission has occurred, such rule, regulation, interpretation, or approval is amended, rescinded, or determined by judicial or other authority to be invalid for any reason.

(f) Any action under this section may be brought in the appropriate United States district court without regard to the amount in controversy, or in any other court of competent jurisdiction. No such action shall be brought later than two years from the date of the occurrence of the violation, except that —

(1) whenever any agency having responsibility for administrative enforcement under section 704 commences an enforcement proceeding within two years from the date of the occurrence of the violation.

(2) whenever the Attorney General commences a civil action under this section within two years from the date of occurrence of the violation, then any applicant who has been a victim of the discrimination which is the subject of such proceeding or civil action may bring an action under this section not later than one year after the commencement of that proceeding or action.

(g) The agencies having responsibility for administrative enforcement under section 704, if unable to obtain compliance with section 701, are authorized to refer the matter to the Attorney General with a recommendation that an appropriate civil action be instituted.

(h) When a matter is referred to the Attorney General pursuant to subsection (g), or whenever he has reason to believe that one or more creditors are engaged in a pattern or practice in violation of this title, the Attorney General may bring a civil action in any appropriate United States district court for such relief as may be appropriate, including injunctive relief.

(i) No person aggrieved by a violation of this title and by a violation of section 805 of the Civil Rights Act of 1968 shall recover under this title and section 812 of the Civil Rights Act of 1968, if such violation is based on the same transaction.

(j) Nothing in this title shall be construed to prohibit the discovery of a creditor's granting standards under appropriate discovery procedures in the court agency in which an action or proceeding is brought. (Amended by Act of 3-23-76, P.L. 94-239, eff. 3-23-76.)

707 Annual Reports to Congress

Annual reports to Congress—Not later than February 1 of each year after 1976, the Board and the Attorney General shall, respectively, make reports to the Congress concerning the administration of their functions under this title, including such recommendations as the Board and the Attorney General, respectively, deem necessary or appropriate. In addition, each report of the Board shall include its assessment of the extent to which compliance with the requirements of this title is being achieved, and a summary of the enforcement actions taken by each of the agencies assigned administrative enforcement responsibilities under section 704. (Amended by Act of 3-23-

76, P.L. 94-239, eff. 2-23-76.)

708 Effective Date

This title takes effect upon the expiration of one year after the date of its enactment. The amendments made by the Equal Credit Opportunity Act Amendments of 1976 shall take effect on the date of enactment thereof and shall apply to any violation occurring on or after such date, except that the amendment made to section 701 of the Equal Credit Opportunity Act shall take effect 12 months after the date of enactment. (Amended by Act of 3-23-76, P.L. 94-239, eff. 2-23-76.)

709 Short Title

This title may be cited as the "Equal Credit Opportunity Act."

Regulation B
Part 202-Equal Credit Opportunity
(12CFR, Part 202, Fed. Reg. 48018)

Table of Contents

Sec.
202.1 Authority, scope, and purpose.

202.2 Definitions.

202.3 Limited exceptions for certain classes of transactions.

202.1 Authority, Scope, and Purpose

(a) Authority and Scope

This regulation is issued by the Board of Governors of the Federal Reserve System pursuant to title VII (Equal Credit Opportunity Act) of the Consumer Credit Protection Act, as amended (15 USC 1601 et seq.). Except as otherwise provided herein, the regulation applies to all persons who are creditors, as defined in 202.2(1). Information collection requirements contained in this regulation have been approved by the Office of Management and Budget under the provisions of 44 USC 3501 et seq. and have been assigned OMB No. 7100-0201.

(b) Purpose

The purpose of this regulation is to promote the availability of credit to all creditworthy applicants without regard to race, color, religion, national origin, sex, marital status, or age (provided the applicant has the capacity to contract); to the fact that all or part of the applicant's income derives from a public assistance program; or to the fact that the applicant has in good faith exercised any right under the Consumer Credit Protection Act. The regulation prohibits creditor practices that discriminate on the basis of any of these factors. The regulation also required creditors to notify applicants of action taken on their applications; to report credit history in the names of both spouses on an account; to retain records of credit applications; and to collect information about the applicant's race and other personal characteristics in applications for certain dwelling-related loans.

202.2 Definitions

For the purposes of this regulation, unless the context indicates otherwise, the following definitions apply.

(a) Account means an extension of credit. When employed in relation to an account, the word use refers only to an open-end credit.

(b) Act means the Equal Credit Opportunity Act (title VII of the Consumer Credit Protection Act).

(c) Adverse Action.

(1) The term means:

(i) A refusal to grant credit in substantially the amount or on substantially the terms requested in an application unless the creditor makes a counteroffer (to grant credit in a different amount or on other terms) and the applicant uses or expressly accepts the credit offered;

(ii) A termination of an account or an unfavorable change in the terms of an account that does not affect all or a substantial portion of a class of the creditor's accounts; or

(iii) A refusal to increase the amount of credit available to an applicant who has made an application for an increase.

(2) The term does not include:

(i) A change in the terms of an account expressly agreed to by an applicant;

(ii) Any action or forbearance relating to an account taken in connection with inactivity, default, or delinquency as to that account;

(iii) A refusal or failure to authorize an account transaction at a point of sale, or loan, except when the refusal is a termination or an unfavorable change in the terms of an account that does not affect all or a substantial portion of a class of the creditor's accounts, or when the refusal is a denial of an application for an increase in the amount of credit available under the account;

(iv) A refusal to extend credit because applicable law prohibits the credit from extending the credit request; or

(v) A refusal to extend credit because the creditor does not offer the type of credit or credit plan requested.

(3) An action that falls within the definition of both paragraphs (c) (1) and (c) (2) of this section is governed by paragraph (c) (2).

(d) Age refers only to the age of natural persons and means the number of fully elapsed years from the date of an applicant's birth.

(e) Applicant means any person who requests or who has received an extension of credit from a creditor, and includes any person who is or may become contractually liable regarding an extension of credit. For purposes of 202.7(d), the term includes guarantors, sureties, endorsers, and similar parties.

(f) Application means an oral or written request for an extension of credit that is made in accordance with procedures established by a creditor for the type of credit requested. The term does not include the use of an account or line of credit to obtain an amount of credit that is within a previously established credit limit. A completed application means an application in connection with which a creditor has received all the information that the creditor regularly obtains and considers in evaluating applications for the amount and type of credit requested from the applicant, and any additional information requested from the applicant, and any approvals or reports by governmental agencies or other persons that are necessary to guarantee, insure, or provide security for the credit or collateral. The creditor shall exercise reasonable diligence in obtaining such information.

(g) Board means the Board of Governors of the Federal Reserve System.

(h) Consumer credit means extended to a natural person primarily for personal, family, or household purposes.

(i) Contractually liable means expressly obligated to

repay all debts arising on an account by reason of an agreement to that effect.

(j) Credit means the right granted by a creditor to an applicant to defer payment of a debt, incur debt and defer its payment, or purchase property or services and defer payment thereof.

(k) Credit card means any card, plate, coupon book, or other single credit device that may be used from time to time to obtain money, property, or services on credit.

(l) Creditor means a person who, in the ordinary course of business, regularly participates in the decision of whether or not to extend credit. The term includes a creditor's assignee, transferee, or subrogee who so participates. For purposes of 202.4 and 202.5(a), the term also includes a person who, in the ordinary course of business, regularly refers applicants or prospective applicants to creditors, or selects or offers to select creditors to whom requests for credit may be made. A person is not a creditor regarding any violation of the act or this regulation committed by another creditor unless the person knew or had reasonable notice of the act, policy, or practice that constituted the violation before becoming involved in the credit transaction. The term does not include a person whose only participation in a credit transaction involves honoring a credit card.

(m) Credit transaction means every aspect of an applicant's dealings with a creditor regarding an application for credit or an existing extension of credit (including, but not limited to, information requirements; investigation procedures; standards of creditworthiness; terms of credit; furnishing of credit information; revocation, alteration, or termination of credit; and collection procedures).

(n) Discriminate against an applicant means to treat an applicant less favorably than other applicants.

(o) Elderly means age 62 or older.

(p) Empirically derived and other credit scoring systems.

(i) A credit scoring system is a system that evaluates an applicant's creditworthiness mechanically, based on key attributes of the applicant and aspects of the transaction, and that determines, alone or in conjunction with an evaluation of additional information about the applicant, whether an applicant is deemed creditworthy. To qualify as an empirically derived, demonstrably and statistically sound credit scoring system, the system must be:

(i) Based on data that are derived from an empirical comparison of sample groups or the population of creditworthy and noncreditworthy applicants who apply for credit within a reasonable preceding period of time;

(ii) Developed for the purpose of evaluating the creditworthiness of applicants with respect to the legitimate business interests of the creditor utilizing the system (including, but not limited to, minimizing bad debt losses and operating expenses in accordance with the creditor's business judgment);

(iii) Developed and validated using accepted statistical principles and methodology and adjusted as necessary to maintain predictive ability.

(2) A creditor may use an empirically derived, demonstrably and statistically sound credit scoring system obtained from another person or may obtain credit experience from which to develop such a system. Any such system must satisfy the criteria set forth in paragraph (p)(1)(i) through (iv) of this section; if the creditor is unable during the development process to validate the system based on its own credit experience in accordance with paragraph (p)(1) of this section, the system must be validated when sufficient credit experience becomes available. A system that fails this validity test is no longer an empirically derived, demonstrably and statistically sound credit scoring system for that creditor.

(q) Extend credit and extension for credit mean the granting of credit in any form (including, but not limited to, credit granted in addition to any existing credit or credit limit; credit granted pursuant to an open-end credit plan; the refinancing or other renewal of credit; including the issuance of a new credit card in place of an expiring credit card or in substitution for an existing credit card; the consolidation of two or more obligations; or the continuance of existing credit without any special effort to collect at or after maturity).

(r) Good faith means honesty in fact in the conduct or transaction.

(s) Inadvertent error means a mechanical, electronic, or clerical error that a creditor demonstrates was not intentional and occurred notwithstanding the maintenance of procedures reasonably adapted to avoid such errors.

(t) Judgmental system of evaluating applicants means any system for evaluating the creditworthiness of an applicant other than an empirically derived, demonstrably and statistically sound credit scoring system.

(u) Marital status means the state of being unmarried, married, or separated, as defined by applicable state law. The term "unmarried" includes persons who are single, divorced, or widowed.

(v) Negative factor or value, in relation to the age of elderly applicants, means utilizing a factor, value, or weight that is less favorable regarding elderly applicants than the creditor's experience warrants or is less favorable than the factor, value, or weight assigned to the class of applicants that are not classified as elderly and are most favored by a creditor on the basis of age.

(w) Open-end credit means credit extended under a plan by which a creditor may permit an applicant to make purchases or obtain loans from time to time directly from the creditor or indirectly by use of a credit card, check, or other device.

(x) Person means a natural person, corporation, government or governmental subdivision or agency, trust, estate, partnership, cooperative, or association.

(y) Pertinent element of creditworthiness, in relation to a judgmental system of evaluating applicants, means any information about applicants that a creditor obtains and considers and that has a demonstrable relationship to a determination of creditworthiness.

(z) Prohibited basis means race, color, religion, national origin, sex, marital status, or age (provided that the applicant has the capacity to enter into a binding contract); the fact that all or part of the applicant's income derives from any public assistance program; or the fact that the applicant has in good faith exercised any right under the Consumer Credit Protection Act or any state law upon which an exemption has been granted by the Board.

(aa) State means any State, the District of Columbia, the Commonwealth of Puerto Rico or any territory or possession of the United States.

202.3 Limited Exceptions for Certain Classes of Transaction

(a) Public utilities credit.

(1) Definition. Public utilities credit refers to extensions of credit that involve public utility services provided through pipe, wire, or other connected facilities, or radio or similar transmissions (including extensions of such facilities), if the charges for service, delayed payment, and any discount for prompt payment are filed with or regulated by a government unit.

(2) Exceptions. The following provisions of this regulation do not apply to public utilities credit:

(i) Section 202.5 (d)(1) concerning information about marital status;

(ii) Section 202.10 relating to furnishing of credit information; and

(iii) Section 202.12(b) relating to record retention.

(b) Securities credit—(l) Definition. Securities credit refers to extensions of credit subject to regulation under section 7 of the Securities Exchange Act of 1934 or extensions of credit by a broker or dealer subject to regulation as a broker or dealer under the Securities Exchange Act of 1934

(2) Exceptions. The following provisions of this regulation do not apply to securities credit:

(i) Section 202.5(c) concerning information about a spouse or former spouse;

(ii) Section 202.5(d)(1) concerning information about marital status;

(iii) Section 202.5(d)(3) concerning information about the sex of an applicant;
(iv) Section 202.7(b) relation to designation of name,

but only to the extent necessary to prevent violation or rules regarding an account in which a broker or dealer has an interest, or rules necessitating the aggregation of accounts of spouses for the purpose of determining controlling interests, beneficial interests, beneficial ownership, or purchase limitations and restrictions;

(v) Section 202.7(c) relating to action concerning open-end accounts, but only to the extent the action taken is on the basis of a change of name or marital status;

(vi) Section 202.7(d) relating to the signature of a spouse or other person;

(vii) Section 202.10 relating to furnishing of credit information; and

(viii) Section 202.12(b) relating to record retention.

(c) Incidental credit. (1) Definition. Incidental credit refers to extensions of consumer credit other than credit of the types described in paragraphs (1) and (b) of this section:

(i) That are not made pursuant to the terms of a credit card account:

(ii) That are not subject to a finance charge (as defined in Regulation Z, 12CFR 226.4); and

(1) That are not payable by agreement in more than four installments.

(2) Exceptions. The following provisions of this regulation do not apply to incidental credit;

(i) Section 202.5(c) concerning information about a spouse or former spouse;

(ii) Section 202.5(d)(1) concerning information about marital status;

(iii) Section 202.5(d)(2) concerning information about income derived from alimony, child support, or separate maintenance payments;

(iv) Section 202.5(d)(3) concerning information about the sex of an applicant, but only to the extent necessary for medical records or similar purposes;

(v) Section 202.7(d) relating to the signature of a spouse or other person;

(vi) Section 202.9 relating to notifications;

(vii) Section 202.10 relating to furnishing of credit information; and

(viii) Section 202.12(b) relation to record retention.

(d) Business credit. (1) Definition. Business credit refers to extensions of credit primarily for business or commercial (including agricultural) purposes, but excluding extensions of credit of the types described in paragraphs (a) and (b) of this section.

(2) Exceptions. The following provisions of this

regulation do not apply to business credit:

(i) Section 202.5(d)(l) concerning information about marital status; and

(ii) Section 202.10 relating to furnishing of credit information.

(3) Modified requirements. The following provisions of this regulation apply to business credit as specified below:

(i) Section 202.9 (a), (b), and (c) relating to notifications; the creditor shall notify the applicant, orally or in writing, of action taken of incompleteness. When credit is denied or when other adverse action is taken, the creditor is required to provide a written statement of the reasons and the ECOA notice specified in section 202.9(b) if the applicant makes a written request for the reasons within 30 days of that notification; and

(ii) Section 202,12(b) relating to record retention; the creditor shall retain records as provided in 202.12(b) if the applicant, within 90 days after being notified of action taken or of incompleteness, requests in writing that records be retained.

(e) Government credit. (1) Definition. Government credit refers to extensions of credit made to governments or governmental subdivisions, agencies, or instrumentalities.

(2) Applicability of regulation. Except for section 202.4 the general rule prohibiting discrimination of a prohibited basis, the requirements of this regulation do not apply to government credit.

202.4 General Rule Prohibiting Discrimination

A creditor shall not discriminate against an applicant on a prohibited basis regarding any aspect of a credit transaction.

202.5 Rules concerning Taking of Applications

(a) Discouraging applications. A creditor shall not make any oral or written statement, in advertising or otherwise, to applicants or prospective applicants that would discourage on a prohibited basis a reasonable person from making or pursuing an application.

(b) General rules concerning requests for information. (1) Except as provided in paragraphs (c) and (d) of this section, a creditor may request any information in connection with an application.

(2) Required collection of information. Notwithstanding paragraphs (c) and (d) of this section, a creditor shall request information for monitoring purposes as required by 202.13 for credit secured by the applicant's dwelling. In addition, a creditor may obtain information required by a regulation, order, or agreement issued by, or entered into with, a court or an enforcement agency (including the Attorney General of the United States or a similar state official) to monitor or enforce compliance with the act, this regulation, or other federal or state statute or regulation.

(3) Specified purpose credit. A creditor may obtain information that is otherwise restricted to determine eligibility for a special purpose credit program, as provided in 202.8(c) and (d).

(c) Information about a spouse or former spouse.

(1) Except as permitted in this paragraph, a creditor may not request any information concerning the spouse or former spouse of an applicant.

(2) Permissible inquiries. A creditor may request any information concerning an applicant's spouse (or former spouse) under paragraph (c)(2)(v) that may be requested about the applicant if —

(i) The spouse will be permitted to use the account;

(ii) The spouse will be contractually liable on the account;

(iii) The applicant is relying on the spouse's income as a basis for repayment of the credit requested;

(iv) The applicant resides in a community property state or property on which the applicant is relying as a basis for repayment of the credit requested is located in such a state; or

(v) The applicant is relying on alimony, child support, or separate maintenance payments from a spouse or former spouse as basis for repayment of the credit requested.

175

(3) Other accounts of the applicant. A creditor may request an applicant to list any account upon which the applicant is liable and to provide the name and address in which the account is carried. A creditor may also ask the names in which an applicant has previously received credit.

(d) Other limitations on information requests.

(1) Marital status. If an applicant applies for individual unsecured credit, a creditor shall not inquire about the applicant's marital status unless the applicant resides in a community property state or is relying on property located in such a state as a basis for repayment of the credit requested. If an application is for other than individual unsecured credit, a creditor may inquire about the applicant's marital status, but shall use only the terms "married," "unmarried," and "separated." A creditor may explain that the category "unmarried" includes single, divorced, and widowed persons.

(2) Disclosure about income from alimony, child support, or separate maintenance. A creditor shall not inquire whether income stated in an application is derived from alimony, child support, or separate maintenance payments unless the creditor discloses to the applicant that such income need not be revealed if the applicant does not want the creditor to consider it in determining the applicant's credit-worthiness.

(3) Sex. A creditor shall not inquire about the sex of

an applicant. An applicant may be requested to designate a title on an application form (such as Ms. Miss, Mr., or Mrs.) If the form discloses that the designation of a title is optional. An applicant form shall otherwise use only terms that are neutral as to sex.

(4) Childbearing, child-rearing. A creditor shall not inquire about birth control practices, intentions concerning the bearing or rearing of children, or capability to bear children. A creditor may inquire about the number and ages of an applicant's dependents or about dependent-related financial obligations or expenditures, provided such information is requested without regard to sex, marital status, or any other prohibited basis.

(5) Race, color, religion, national origins. A creditor shall not inquire about the race, color, religion, or national origin of an applicant or any other person in connection with a credit transaction. A creditor may inquire about an applicant's permanent residence and immigration status.

(e) Written applications. A creditor shall take written applications for the types of credit covered by 202.13 (a), but need not take written applications for other types of credit.

202.6 Rules concerning Evaluation of Applications

(a) General rule concerning use of information. Except as otherwise provided in the act and this regulation, a creditor may consider information obtained, so long as the information is not used to discriminate against an applicant on a prohibited basis.

(b) Specific rules concerning use of information.

(1) Except as provided in the act and this regulation, a creditor shall not take a prohibited basis into account in any system of evaluating the creditworthiness of applicants.

(2) Age, receipt of public assistance. (i) Except as permitted in this paragraph (b) (2), a creditor shall not take into account an applicant's age (provided that the applicant has the capacity to enter into a binding contract) or whether an applicant's income derives from any public assistance program.

(ii) In an empirically derived, demonstrably and statistically sound credit scoring system, a creditor may use an applicant's age as a predictive variable, provided that the age of an elderly applicant is not assigned a negative factor or value.

(iii) In a judgmental system of evaluating creditworthiness, a creditor may consider an applicant's age or whether an applicant's income derives from any public assistance program only for the purposes of determining a pertinent element of creditworthiness.

(iv) In any system of evaluating creditworthiness, a creditor may consider the age of an elderly applicant when such age is used to favor the elderly applicant in extending credit.

178

(3) Childbearing, child-rearing. In evaluating credit-worthiness, a creditor shall not use assumptions or aggregate statistics relating to the likelihood that any group of persons will bear or rear children or will, for that reason, receive diminished or interrupted income in the future.

(4) Telephone listing. A creditor shall not take into account whether there is a telephone listing in the name of applicant for consumer credit, but may take into account whether there is a telephone in the applicant's residence.

(5) Income. A creditor shall not discount or exclude from consideration the income of an applicant or the spouse of an applicant because of a prohibited basis or because the income is derived from part-time employment or is an annuity, pension, or other retirement benefit; a creditor may consider the amount and probable continuance of any income in evaluating an applicant's creditworthiness. When an applicant relies on alimony, child support, or separate maintenance payments in applying for credit, the creditor shall consider such payments as income to the extent that they are likely to be consistently made.

(6) Credit history. To the extent that a creditor considers credit history in evaluating the creditworthiness of similarly qualified applicants for a similar type and amount of credit, in evaluating an applicant's creditworthiness a creditor shall consider:

(i) The credit history, when available, of accounts

179

designated as accounts that the applicant and the applicant's spouse are permitted to use or for which they are contractually liable:

(ii) On the applicant's request, any information the applicant may present that tends to indicate that the credit history being considered by the creditor does not accurately reflect the applicant's creditworthiness; and

(iii) On the applicant's request, the credit history, when available, of any account reported in the name of the applicant's spouse or former spouse that the applicant can demonstrate accurately reflects the applicant's creditworthiness.

(7) Immigration status. A creditor may consider whether an applicant is a permanent resident of the United States, the applicant's immigration status, and any additional information that may be necessary to ascertain the creditor's rights and remedies regarding repayment.

(c) State property laws. A creditor's consideration or application of state laws directly or indirectly affecting creditworthiness does not constitute unlawful discrimination for the purposes of the act or this regulation.

202.7 Rules concerning Extensions of Credits

(a) Individual accounts. A creditor shall not refuse to grant an individual account to a creditworthy applicant on the basis of sex, marital status, or any other prohibited basis.

(b) Designation of name. A creditor shall not refuse to allow an applicant to open or maintain an account in a birth-given first name and a surname that is the applicant's birth-given surname, the spouse's surname, or combined surname.

(c) Action concerning existing open-end accounts.

(1) Limitations. In the absence of the applicant's inability or unwillingness to repay, a creditor shall not take any of the following actions regarding an applicant who is contractually liable on an existing open-end account on the basis of the applicant's reaching a certain age or retiring or on the basis of a change in the applicant's name or marital status:

(i) Require a reapplication, except as provided in paragraph (c)(2) of this section;

(ii) Change the terms of the account; or

(iii) Terminate the account.

(2) Requiring reapplication. A creditor may require a reapplication for an open-end account on the basis of a change in the marital status of an applicant who is contractually liable if the credit granted was based in whole or in part on income of the applicant's spouse and if information available to the creditor indicates that the applicant's income may not support the amount of credit currently available.

(d) Signature of spouse or other person. (1) Rule for

qualified applicant. Except as provided in this paragraph, a creditor shall not require the signature of an applicant's spouse or other person other than a joint applicant, on any credit instrument if the applicant qualified under the creditor's standards of creditworthiness for the amount and terms of the credit requested.

(2) Unsecured credit. If an applicant requests credit and relies in part upon property that the applicant owns jointly with another person to satisfy the creditor's standards of creditworthiness, the creditor may require the signature of the other person only on the instruments necessary, or reasonably believed by the creditor to be necessary, under the law of the state in which the property is located, to enable the creditor to reach the property being relied upon in the event of the death or default of the applicant.

(3) Unsecured credit-community property states. If a married applicant requests unsecured credit and resides in a community property state, or if the property upon which the applicant is relying is located in such a state, a creditor may require the signature of the spouse on any instrument necessary, or reasonably believed by the creditor to be necessary, under applicable state law to make the community property available to satisfy the debt in the event of default if:

(i) Applicable state law denies the applicant power to manage or control sufficient community property to qualify for the amount of credit requested under the creditor's standards of creditworthiness; and

(ii) The applicant does not have sufficient separate

property to qualify for the amount of credit requested without regard to community property.

(4) Secured credit. If an applicant requests secured
credit, a creditor may require the signature of the
applicant's spouse or other person on any instrument
necessary, or reasonably believed by the creditor to
be necessary, under applicable state law to make the
property being offered as security available to satisfy the debt in the event of default, for example, an
instrument to create a valid lien, pass clear title,
waive inchoate rights or assign earnings.

(5) Additional parties. If, under a creditor's standards
of creditworthiness, the personal liability of an additional party is necessary to support the extension of
the credit requested, a creditor may request a cosigner, a guarantor, or the like. The applicant's spouse
may serve as an additional party, but the creditor shall
not require that the spouse be the additional party.

(6) Rights of additional parties. A creditor shall not
impose requirements upon an additional party that
the creditor is prohibited from imposing upon an
applicant under this section.

(e) Insurance. A creditor shall not refuse to extend
credit and shall not terminate an account because
credit life, health, accident, disability, or other credit-related insurance is not available on the basis of
the applicant's age.

202.8 Special Purpose Credit Programs

(a) Standards for programs. Subject to the provisions of paragraph (b) of this section, the act and this regulation permit a creditor to extend special purpose credit to applicants who meet eligibility requirements under the following types of credit programs:

(1) Any credit assistance program expressly authorized by federal or state law for the benefit of an economically disadvantaged class or persons;

(2) Any credit assistance program offered by a not-for-profit organization as defined under section 801(c) of the Internal Revenue Code of 1954, as amended, for the benefit of its members or for the benefit of an economically disadvantaged class of persons participates to meet special social needs, if —

(i) The program is established and administered pursuant to a written plan that identifies the class of persons that the program is designed to benefit and sets forth the procedures and standards for extending credit pursuant to the program; and

(ii) The program is established and administered to extend credit to a class of persons, who, under the organization's customary standards of creditworthiness, probably would not receive such credit or would receive it on less favorable terms than are ordinarily available to other applicants applying to the organization for a similar type and amount of credit.

(b) Rules in other sections. (1) General applicability.

All of the provisions of this regulation apply to each of the special purpose credit programs described in paragraph (a) of this section unless modified by this section.

(2) Common characteristics. A program described in paragraph (a)(2) or (a)(3) of this section qualifies as a special purpose credit program only if it was established and is administered so as not to discriminate against an applicant on any prohibited basis; however, all program participants may be required to share one or more common characteristics (for example, race, national origin, or sex) so long as the program was not established and is not administered with the purpose of evading the requirements of the act or this regulation.

(c) Special rule concerning requests and use of information. If participants in a special purpose credit program described in paragraph (a) of this section are required to possess one or more common characteristics (for example, race, national origin, or sex) and if the program otherwise satisfies the requirements of paragraph (a) of this section, a creditor may request and consider information regarding the common characteristics in determining the applicant's eligibility for the program.

(d) Special rule in the case of financial need. If financial need is one of the criteria under a special purpose program described in paragraph (a) of this section, the creditor may request and consider, in determining an applicant's eligibility for the program, information regarding the applicant's martial status, alimony, child support, and separate maintenance income; and the spouse's financial resources. In addition, a creditor may obtain the signature of an applicant's spouse or other person on an application or credit instrument relating to a special purpose program if the signature is required by federal or state law.

202.9 Notifications

(a) Notification of action taken, ECOA notice, and statement of specific reasons (1) When notification is required. A creditor shall notify an applicant of action taken within:

(i) 30 days after receiving a completed application concerning the creditor's approval of, counteroffer to, or adverse action on the application;

(ii) 30 days after taking adverse action on an incomplete application, unless notice is provided in accordance with paragraph (c) of this section;

(iii) 30 days after taking adverse action on an existing account; or

(iv) 90 days after notifying the applicant or a counteroffer if the applicant does not expressly accept or use the credit offered.

(2) Content of notification when adverse action is taken. A notification given to an applicant when adverse action is taken shall be in writing and shall contain: A statement of the action taken; the name

and address of the creditor; a statement of the provisions of section 701(a) of the act; the name and address of the federal agency that administers compliance with respect to the creditor; and either:

(i) A statement of specific reasons for the action taken; or

(ii) A disclosure of the applicant's right to a statement of specific reasons with 30 days, if the statement is requested within 60 days of the creditor's notification. The disclosure shall include the name, address, and telephone number of the person or office from which the statement of reasons can be obtained. If the creditor chooses to provide the reasons orally, the creditor shall also disclose the applicant's right to have them confirmed in writing within 30 days of receiving a written request for confirmation from the applicant.

(b) Form of ECOA notice and statement of specific reasons.

(1) ECOA notice. To satisfy the disclosure requirements of paragraph (a)(2) of this section regarding section 701(a) of the act, the creditor shall provide a notice that is substantially similar to the following: The Federal Equal Credit Opportunity Act prohibits creditors from discriminating against credit applicants on the basis of race, color, religion, national origin, sex, marital status, age (provided the applicant has the capacity to enter into a binding contract); because all or part of the applicant's income derives from public assistance programs; or because

187

the applicant has in good faith exercised any right under the Consumer Credit Protection Act. The federal agency then administers compliance with this law concerning this creditor is (name and address as specified by the appropriate agency listed in Appendix A of this regulation).

(2) Statement of specific reasons. The statement of reasons for adverse action required by paragraph (a)(2)(i) of this section must be specific and indicate the principal reason(s) for the adverse action. Statements that the adverse action was based on the creditor's internal standards policies or that the applicant failed to achieve the qualifying score on the creditor's credit scoring system are insufficient.

(c) Incomplete applications. (1) Notice alternatives. Within 30 days after receiving an application that is incomplete regarding matters that an applicant can complete, the creditor shall notify the applicant either:

(i) Of action taken, in accordance with paragraph (a) of this section; or

(ii) Of the incompleteness, in accordance with paragraph (c)(2) of this section.

(2) Notice of incompleteness. If additional information is needed from an applicant, the creditor shall send a written notice to the applicant specifying the information needed, designating a reasonable period of time for the applicant to provide the information, and informing the applicant that failure to provide the information will result in no further consideration being given to the application. The creditor shall have no further obligation under this section if the applicant fails to respond within the designated time period. If the applicant supplies the requested information within the designated time period, the creditor shall take action on the application and notify the applicant in accordance with paragraph (a) of this section.

(3) Oral requests for information. At its option, a creditor may inform the applicant orally of the need for additional information; but if the application remains incomplete the creditor shall send a notice in accordance with paragraph (c)(1) of this section.

(4) Oral notifications by small-volume creditors. The requirements of this section (including statements of specific reasons) are satisfied by oral notifications in the case of any creditor that did not receive more than 150 applications during the preceding calendar year.

(e) Withdrawal of approved applications. When an applicant submits an application and the parties contemplate that the applicant will inquire about its status, if the creditor approves the application and the applicant has not inquired within 30 days after applying, the creditor may treat the application as withdrawn and need not comply with paragraph (a)(1) of this section.

(f) Multiple applicants. When an application involves more than one applicant, notification need

only by given to one of them, but must be given to
the primary applicant where one is readily apparent.

(g) Applications submitted through a third party.
When an application is made on behalf of an applicant to more than one creditor and the applicant
expressly accepts or uses credit offered by one of the
creditors, notification of action taken by any of the
other creditors is not required. If no credit is offered
or if the applicant does not expressly accept or use
any credit offered, each creditor taking adverse
action must comply with this section, directly or
through a third party. A notice given by a third party
shall disclose the identity of each creditor on whose
behalf the notice is given.

202.10 Furnishing of Credit Information

(a) Designation of accounts. A creditor that furnished credit information shall designate:

(1) Any new account to reflect the participation of
both spouses if the applicant's spouse is permitted to
use or is contractually liable on the account (other
than as a guarantor, surety, endorser, or similar
party);

(2) Any existing account to reflect such participation, within 90 days after receiving a written request
to do so from one of the spouses.

(b) Routine reports to consumer reporting agency. If
a creditor furnishes credit information to a consumer
reporting agency concerning an account designated

to reflect the participation of both spouses, the creditor shall furnish the information in a manner that will enable the agency to provide access to the information in the name of each spouse.

(c) Reporting in response to inquiry. If a creditor furnishes credit information in response to an inquiry concerning an account designated to reflect the participation of both spouses, the creditor shall furnish the information in the name of the spouse about whom the information is requested.

202.11 Relations to State Law

(a) Inconsistent state laws. Except as otherwise provided in this section, this regulation alters, affects, or preempts only those state laws that are inconsistent with the act and this regulation and then only to the extent of the inconsistency. A state law is not inconsistent if it is more protective of an applicant.

(b) Preempted provisions of state law. (1) A state law is deemed to be inconsistent with the requirements of the act and this regulation and less protective of an applicant within the meaning of section 706(f) of the act to the extent that the law:

(i) Requires or permits a practice or act prohibited by the act or this regulation;

(ii) Prohibits the individual extension of consumer credit to both parties to a marriage if each spouse individually and voluntarily applies for such credit;

(iii) Prohibits inquiries or collection of data required to comply with the act or this regulation;

(iv) Prohibits asking or considering age in an empirically derived, demonstrably and statistically sound credit scoring system to determine a pertinent element of creditworthiness, or to favor an elderly applicant; or

(v) Prohibits inquiries necessary to establish or administer as special purpose credit program as defined by 202.8.

(2) A creditor, state, or other interested party may request the Board to determine whether a state law is inconsistent with the requirements of the act and this regulation.

(c) Laws on finance charges, loan ceilings. If married applicants voluntarily apply for and obtain individual accounts with the same creditor, the accounts shall not be aggregated or otherwise combined for purposes of determining permissible finance charges or loan ceilings under any federal or state law. Permissible loan ceiling laws shall be construed to permit each spouse to become individually liable up to the amount of the loan ceilings, less the amount for which the applicant is jointly liable.

(d) State and federal laws not affected. This section does not alter or annul any provision of state property laws, laws relating to the disposition of decedents' estates, or federal or state banking regulation directed only toward insuring the solvency of financial institutions.

(e) Exemption for state-regulated transactions.

(1) Applications. A state may apply to the Board for an exemption from the requirements of the act and this regulation for any class of credit transactions within the state. The Board will grant such an exemption if the Board determines that:

(i) The class of credit transactions is subject to state law requirements substantially similar to the act and this regulation or that applicants are afforded greater protection under state law; and

(ii) There is adequate provision for state enforcement.

(2) Liability and enforcement. (i) No exemption will extend to the civil liability provisions of section 706 or the administrative enforcement provisions of section 704 of the act.

(ii) After an exemption has been granted, the requirements of the applicable state law (except for additional requirements not imposed by federal law) will constitute the requirements of the act and this regulation.

202.12 Record Retention

(a) Retention of prohibited information. A creditor may retain in its files information that is prohibited by the act or this regulation in evaluating applications, without violating the act or this regulation, if

the information is obtained:
(1) From any source prior to March 23, 1977;

(2) From consumer reporting agencies, an applicant, or others without the specific request of the creditor; or

(3) As required to monitor compliance with the act and this regulation or other federal or state statutes or regulations.

(b) Preservation of records. (1) Applications. For 25 months after the date that a creditor notifies an applicant of action taken on an application or incompleteness, the creditor shall retain in original form or a copy thereof —

(i) any application that it receives, any information required to be obtained concerning characteristics of the applicant to monitor compliance with the act and this regulation or other similar law, and any other written or recorded information used in evaluating the application and not returned to the applicant at the applicant's request;

(ii) A copy of the following documents if furnished to the applicant in written form (or, if furnished orally, any notation or memorandum made by the creditor):

(A) The notification of action taken; and

(B) The statement of specific reasons for adverse action; and

(iii) Any written statement submitted by the applicants alleging a violation of the act or this regulation.

(2) Existing accounts. For 25 months after the date that a creditor notifies an applicant of adverse action regarding an existing account, the creditor shall retain as to that account, in original form or a copy thereof —

(i) Any written or recorded information concerning the adverse action: and

(ii) Any written statement submitted by the applicant alleging a violation of the act or this regulation.

(3) Other applications. For 25 months after the date that a creditor receives an application for which the creditor is not required to comply with the notification requirements of 202.9, the creditor shall retain all written or recorded information in its possession concerning the applicant, including any notation of action taken.

(4) Enforcement of proceedings and investigations. A creditor shall retain the information specified in this section beyond 25 months if it has actual notice that it is under investigation or is subject to an enforcement proceeding for an alleged violation of the act of this violation of the act or this regulation by the Attorney General of the United States or by an enforcement agency charged with monitoring that creditor's compliance with the act and this regulation, or if it has been served with notice of an action filed pursuant to section 706 of the act and 202.14 of this regulation. The creditor shall retain the information until final disposition of the matter, unless an earlier time is allowed by order of the agency or court.

202.13 Information for Monitoring Purposes

(a) Information to be requested. A creditor that receives an application for credit primarily for the purchase or refinancing of a dwelling occupied by the applicant as a principal residence, where the extension of credit will be secured by the dwelling, shall request as part of the application the following information regarding the applicant(s):

(1) Race or national origin, using the categories American Indian or Alaskan Native; Asian or Pacific Islander; Black; White; Hispanic; Other (specify);

(2) Sex;

(3) Marital status, using the categories married, unmarried, and separated; and

(4) Age.
"Dwelling" means a residential structure that contains one to four units, whether or not that structure is attached to real property. The term includes, but is not limited to, an individual condominium or cooperative unit, and a mobile or other manufactured home.

(b) Obtaining of information. Questions regarding race or national origin, sex, martial status, and age may be listed, at the creditor's option, on the application form or on a separate form that refers to the application. The applicant(s) shall be asked but not required to supply the requested information. If the applicant(s) chooses not to provide the information or any part of it, that fact shall be noted on the form. The creditor shall then also note on the form, to the extent possible, the race or national origin and sex of the applicant(s) on the basis of visual observation or surname.

(c) Disclosure to applicant(s). The creditor shall inform the applicant(s) that the information regarding race or national origin, sex, marital status, and age is being requested by the federal government for the purpose of monitoring compliance with federal statutes that prohibit creditors from discriminating against applicants on those bases. The creditor shall also inform the applicant(s) that if the applicant(s) chooses not to provide the information, the creditor is required to note the race or national origin and sex on the basis of visual observation or surname.

(d) Substitutive-monitoring program. A monitoring program required by an agency charged with administrative enforcement under section 704 of the act may be substituted for the requirements contained in paragraphs (a), (b), and (c).

202.14 Enforcement, Penalties, and Liabilities

(a) Administrative enforcement. (1) As set forth more fully in section 704 of the act, administrative enforcement of the act and this regulation regarding certain creditors is assigned to the Comptroller the Currency, Board of Governors of the Federal Reserve System, Board of Directors of the Federal Deposit Insurance Corporation, Federal Home Loan Bank Board (acting directly or through the Federal Savings and Loan Insurance Corporation), National Credit Union Administration, Interstate Commerce Commission, Secretary of Agriculture, Farm Credit Administration, Securities and Exchange Commission, Small Business Administration, and Secretary of Transportation.

(2) Except to the extent that administrative enforcement is specifically assigned to other authorities, compliance with the requirements imposed under the act and this regulation is enforced by the Federal Trade Commission.

(b) Penalties and Liabilities. (1) Sections 706(a) and (b) and 702(g) of the act provide that any creditor that fails to comply with a requirement imposed by the act or this regulation is subject to civil liability for actual and punitive damages in individual or class actions. Pursuant to sections 704(b), (c), and (d) and 702(g) of the act, violations of the act or regulations also constitute violations of other federal laws. Liability for punitive damages is restricted to nongovernmental entities and is limited to $10,000 in individual actions and the lesser of $50,000 or 1 percent of the creditor's net worth in class actions, section 706(c) provides for equitable and declaratory relief and section 706(d) authorizes the awarding of costs and reasonable attorney's fees to an aggrieved applicant in a successful action.

(2) As provided in section 706(f), a civil action under the act or this regulation may be brought in the appropriate United States district court without regard to the amount in controversy or in any other court of competent jurisdiction within two years after the date of the occurrence of the violation, or within one year after the commencement of an administrative enforcement proceeding or of a civil action brought by the Attorney General of the United States within two years after the alleged violation.

(3) Sections 706(g) and (h) provide that, if an agency responsible for administrative enforcement is unable to obtain compliance with the act or this regulation, it may refer the matter to the Attorney General of the United States. On referral, or whenever the Attorney General has reason to believe that one or more creditors are engaged in a pattern or practice in violation of the act or this regulation, the Attorney General may bring a civil action.

(c) Failure of compliance. A creditor's failure to comply with 202.6(b)(6), 202.9, 202.10, 202.12 or 202.13 is not a violation if it results from an inadvertent error. On discovering an error under 202.9 and 202.10, the creditor shall correct it as soon as possible. If a creditor inadvertently obtains the monitoring information regarding the race or national origin and sex of the applicant in a dwelling-related transaction not covered by 202.13, the creditor may act on and retain the application without violating the regulation.

Appendix A: Federal Enforcement Agencies

The following list indicates the federal agencies that enforce Regulation B for particular classes of creditors. Any questions concerning a particular creditor should be directed to its enforcement agency.

National banks
Comptroller of the Currency
Consumer Examinations Division
Washington, D.C. 20219

State member banks
Federal Reserve Bank serving the district in which the state member bank is located.

Nonmember insured banks
Federal Deposit Insurance Corporation Regional Director for the region in which the nonmember insured bank is located.

Savings institutions insured by the FSLIC and members for the FHLB system (except for savings banks insured by FDIC):
The Federal Home Loan Bank Board Supervisory Agent in the district in which the institution is located.

Federal credit unions
Regional Office of the National Credit Union Administration serving the area in which the federal credit union is located.

Creditors subject to Interstate Commerce Commission
Office Proceedings
Interstate Commerce Commission
Washington, D.C. 20523

Creditors subject to Packers and Stockyards Act:
Nearest Packers and Stockyards Administration area
supervisor

U.S. Small Business Administration
1441 L Street, N.W.
Washington, D.C. 20416

APPENDIX C

Fair Debt Collection
Practices Act
Consumer Credit
Protection Act

(PUBLIC LAW 15 USC 1601 et seq.)
CONSUMER CREDIT PROTECTION ACT

An act to amend The Consumer Credit Protection
Act to prohibit abusive practices by debt collectors.

Be it enacted by the Senate and House of
Representatives of The United States of America in
Congress assembled, That the Consumer Credit
Protection Act (15 U.S.C. 1601 et seq.) is amended
by adding at the end thereof the following new title:

TITLE VIII
DEBT COLLECTION PRACTICES

801. Short title
802. Findings and purpose
803. Definitions
804. Acquisition of location information
**805. Communication in connection with debt col-
lection**

Section 801 Short Title

> This title may be cited as the "Fair Debt Collection Practice Act."

Section 802 Findings and purpose

> (a) There is an abundant evidence of the users' abusive, deceptive, and unfair debt collectors. Abusive debt collection practices contribute to the number of personal bankruptcies, to martial instability, to the loss of jobs, and to invasions of privacy.

> (b) Existing laws and procedures for redressing these inquiries are inadequate to protect consumers.

> (c) Means other than misrepresentation or other abusive debt collection practices are available for the effective collection of debts.

> (d) Abusive debt collection practices are carried on to a substantial extent in interstate commerce and through means and instrumentalities of such com-

merce. Even where abusive debt collection practices are purely intrastate in character, they nevertheless directly affect interstate commerce.

(e) It is the purpose of this title to eliminate abusive debt collection practices by debt collectors, to insure that those debt collectors who refrain from using abusive debt collection practices are not competitively disadvantaged, and to promote consistent State action to protect consumers against debt collection abuses.

Section 803 Definitions

As used in this title —

(1) The term "Commission" means the Federal Trade Commission.

(2) The term "communication" means the conveying of information regarding a debt directly or indirectly to any person through any medium.

(3) The term "consumer" means any natural person obligated or allegedly obligated to pay any debt.

(4) The term "creditor" means any person who offers or extends credit creating a debt or to whom a debt is owed, but such an assignment or transfer of a debt in default solely for the purpose of facilitating collection of such debt for another.

(5) The term "debt" means any obligation or alleged obligation of a consumer to pay money arising out

of a transaction in which the money, property, insurance, or services which are the subject of the transaction are primarily for personal, family, or household purposes, whether or not such obligation has been reduced to judgment.

(6) The term "debt collector" means any person who uses any instrumentality of interstate commerce or the mails on any business the principal purpose of which is the collection of any debts, or who regularly collects or attempts to collect, directly or indirectly, debts owed or due or asserted to be owed or due another. Notwithstanding the exclusion provided by clause (G) of the last sentence of this paragraph, the term includes any creditor who, in the process of collecting his own debts, uses any name other than his own which would indicate that a third person is collecting or attempting to collect such debts. For the purpose of section 808(G), such term also includes any person who uses any instrumentality of interstate commerce or the mails on any business the principal purpose of which is the enforcement for security interest. The term does not include —

(A) any officer or employee of a creditor while, in the name of the creditor, collecting debts for such creditor;

(B) any person while acting as a debt collector for another person, both of who are related by common ownership or affiliated by corporate control, if the person acting as a debt collector does so only for the persons to whom it is to related or affiliated and if the principal business of such person is not the collection of debts;

206

(C) any officer or employee of the United States or any State to the extent that collecting or attempting to collect any debt is in the performance of his official duties;

(D) any person while serving or attempting to serve legal process on any other person in connection with the judicial enforcement of any debt;

(E) any nonprofit organization which, at the request of consumers, performs bona fide consumer credit counseling and assists consumers in the liquidation of their debts by receiving payments from such consumers and distributing such amounts to creditors;

(F) any attorney-at-law collecting a debt as an attorney on behalf of and in the name of a client; and

(G) any person collecting or attempting to collect any debt owed or due or asserted to be owed or due another to the extent such activity (i) is incidental to a bona fide fiduciary obligation or a bona fide escrow arrangement; (ii) concerns a debt which was originated by such a person; (iii) concerns a debt which was not in default at the time it was obtained by such person; or (iv) concerns a debt obtained by such a person as a secured party in commercial credit transaction involving the creditor.

(7) The term "location information" means a consumer's place of abode and his telephone number at such place, or his place of employment.

(8) The term "State" means any State, territory, or

possession of the United States, the District of Columbia, the Commonwealth of Puerto Rico, or any political subdivision of any of the foregoing.

Section 804 Acquisition of Location Information

Any debt collector communicating with any person other than the consumer for the purpose of acquiring location information about the consumer shall —

(1) indemnify himself, state that he is confirming or correcting location information concerning the consumer, and, only if expressly requested, identify his employer;

(2) not state that such consumer owes any debts;

(3) not communicate with any such person more than once unless requested to do so by such person or unless the debt collector reasonably believes that the earlier response of such person is erroneous or incomplete and that such person now has correct or compete location information;

(4) not communicate by postcard;

(5) not use any language or symbol on any envelope or in the contents of any communication effected by the mails or telegram that indicates that the debt collector is in the debt collection of a debt; and

(6) after the debt collector knows the consumer is represented by an attorney with regard to the subject debt and has knowledge of, or can readily ascertain,

such attorney's name and address, not communicate with any person other than that attorney, unless the attorney fails to respond within a reasonable period of time to communicate with the debt collector.

Section 805 Communication with Debt Collection

(a) Communication with the consumer generally, without the prior consent of the consumer given directly to the debt collector or the express permission of a court of competent jurisdiction, a debt collector may not communicate with a consumer with the collection for any debt —

(1) At any unusual item or place or a time or place known or which should be known to be inconvenient to the consumer. In the absence of knowledge or circumstances to the contrary, a debt collector shall assume that the convenient time for communicating with a consumer is after 8 o'clock anti-meridian and before 9 o'clock post-meridian, local time at the consumer's location;

(2) if the debt collector knows the consumer is represented by an attorney with respect to such debt and has knowledge of, or can readily ascertain such attorney's address, unless the attorney fails to respond within a reasonable period of time to a communication from the debt collector or unless the attorney consents to direct communication with the consumer; or

(3) at the consumer's place of employment if the debt collector knows or has reason to know that the

consumer's employer prohibits the consumer from receiving such communication.

(b) Communication with third parties. Except as provided in section 804, without the prior consent of the consumer given directly to the debt collector, or the express permission of a court of competent jurisdiction, or as reasonably necessary to effectuate a post-judgment judicial remedy, a debt collector may not communicate, in connection with the collection of any debt, with any other person other than the consumer, his attorney, a consumer reporting agency if otherwise permitted by law, the creditor, the attorney of the creditor, or the attorney of the debt collector.

(c) Ceasing communication. If a consumer notifies a debt collector in writing that the consumer refuses to pay a debt or that the consumer wishes the debt collector to cease further communication with the consumer, the debt collector shall not communicate further with the consumer with respect to such debt, except —

(1) to advise the consumer that the debt collector's further efforts are being terminated;

(2) to notify the consumer that the debt collector or creditor may invoke specified remedies which are ordinarily invoked by such debt collector or creditor; or

(3) where applicable, to notify the consumer that the debt collector or creditor intends to invoke a specific remedy.

If such notice from the consumer is made by mail, notification shall be complete upon receipt.

(d) For the purpose of this selection, the term "consumer" includes the consumer's spouse, parent (if the consumer is a minor), guardian, executor, or administrator.

Section 806 Harassment or Abuse

A debt collector may not engage in any conduct the natural consequence of which is to harass, oppress, or abuse any person in connection with collection of a debt. Without limiting the general application of the foregoing, the following conduct is a violation of this section:

(1) The use or threat of violence or other criminal means to harm the physical person, reputation, or property of any person.

(2) The use of obscene or profane language or language the natural consequence of which is to abuse the hearer or the reader.

(3) The publication of a list of customers who allegedly refuse to pay debts, except a consumer reporting agency or to persons meeting the requirements of section 803(f) or 804(3) of this Act.

(4) The advertisement for sale of any debt to coerce payment of the debt.

(5) Causing a telephone to ring or engaging in any tele-

phone conversation repeatedly or continuously with intent to annoy, abuse, or harass any person at the called number.

(6) Except as provided in section 804, the placement of telephone calls without meaningful disclosure to the caller's identity.

Section 807 False or Misleading Representations

A debt collector may not use any false, deceptive, or misleading representation or means in connection with the collection of any debt.

Without limiting the general application of the foregoing, the following conduct is a violation of this section:

(1) The false representation or implication that the debt collector is vouched for, bonded by, or affiliated with the United States or any State, including the use of any badge, uniform, or facsimile thereof.

(2) The false representation of —

(A) the character amount, or legal status of any debt, or

(B) any services rendered or compensation which may be lawfully received by any debt collector for the collection of a debt.

(3) The false representation or implication that any individual is an attorney or that any communication is from an attorney.

212

(4) The representation or implication that nonpayment of any debt will result in the arrest or imprisonment of any person or the seizure, garnishment, attachment, or sale of any property or wages of any person unless such action is lawful and the debt collector or creditor intends to take such action.

(5) The threat to take any action that cannot legally be taken or that is not intended to be taken.

(6) The false representation or implication that a sale, referral, or other transfer of any interest in a debt shall cause the consumer to —

(A) lose any claim or defense to payment of the debt; or

(B) become subject to any practices prohibited by this title

(7) The false representation or implication that the consumer committed any crime or any conduct in order to disgrace the consumer.

(8) Communicating or threatening to communicate to any person credit information which is known or which should be known to be false, including the failure to communicate that a disputed debt is disputed.

(9) The use or distribution of any written communication which simulates or is falsely represented to be a document authorized issued, or approved by any court, official, or agency of the United States or any State, or which create a false impression as to its source, authorization, or approval.

(10) The use of any false representation or deceptive means to collect, or attempt to collect, any debt or to obtain information concerning a consumer.

(11) Except as otherwise provided for communications to acquire location information under section 804, failure to disclose clearly in all communications made to collect a debt or to obtain information about a consumer, that debt collector is attempting to collect a debt and that any information obtained will be used for that purpose.

(12) The false representation or implication that accounts have been turned over to innocent purchasers for value.

(13) The false representation or implication the documents are legal process.

(14) The use of any business, company, or organization name other than the true name of the debt collector's business, company, or any other organization.

(15) The false representation or implication that documents are not legal process forms or do not require action by the consumer.
(16) The false representation or implication that a debt collector operates or is employed by a consumer reporting agency as defined by section 603 (f) of this Act.

Section 808 Unfair Practices

A debt collector may not use unfair or unconscionable means to collect or attempt to collect any debt. Without limiting the general application of the foregoing, the following conduct is a violation of this section:

(1) The collection if any amount including any interest, fee, charge, or expense incidental to the principal obligation unless such amount is expressly authorized by the agreement creating the debt or permitted by law.

(2) The acceptance by a debt collector from any person of a check or other payment instrument postdated by more than five days unless such person is notified in writing of the debt collector's intent to deposit such check or instrument not more than ten nor less than three business days prior to such deposit.

(3) The solicitation by a debt collector of any postdated check or other postdated payment instrument purpose of threatening or instituting criminal prosecution.

(4) Depositing or threatening to deposit any postdated check or other postdated payment instrument prior to the date on such check or instrument.

(5) Causing charges to be made to any person for communications by concealment of the true purpose of the communication. Such charges include, but are not limited to, collect telephone calls or telegram fees.

215

(6) Talking or threatening to take any non-judicial action to effect dispossession or disablement of the property if —

(A) there is no present right to the property claimed as collateral through an enforceable security interest;

(B) there is no present limitation to take possession of the property; or

(C) the property is exempt by law from such dispossession or disablement.

(7) Communicating with a consumer regarding a debt by postcard.

(8) Using any language or symbol, other than the debt collector's address, on any envelope when communicating with a consumer by use of the mails or by telegram, except that a debt collector may use his business name if such name does not indicate that he is in the debt collection business.

Section 809 Validation of Debts

(a) Within five days after the initial communication with a consumer in connection with the collection of any debt, a debt collector shall, unless the following information is contained in the initial communication, or the consumer has paid the debt, send the consumer a written notice containing —

(1) the amount of the debt;

(2) the name of the creditor to whom it is owed;

(3) a statement that unless the consumer, within thirty days after receipt of the notice, disputes the validity of the debt, or any portion thereof, the debt will be assumed to be valid by the debt collector.

(4) a statement that if the consumer notifies the debt collector in writing within the thirty-day period that the debt, or any portion thereof is disputed, the debt collector will obtain verification of the debt or a copy of a judgment against the consumer by debt collector; and

(5) a statement that, upon the consumer's written request within the thirty-day period, the debt collector will provide the consumer with the name and address of the original creditor, if different from the current creditor.

(b) If the consumer notifies the debt collector in writing within the thirty-day period described in subsection (a) that the debt, or any portion thereof, is disputed, or that the consumer requests the name and address of the original creditor, the debt collector shall cease collection of the debt, or any disputed portion thereof, until the debt collector obtains verification or judgment, or the name and address of the original creditor, and a copy of such verification or judgment, or the name and address of the original creditor, is mailed by the consumer by the debt collector.

(c) The failure of a consumer to dispute the validity

of a debt under this section may not be construed by any court as an admission of liability by the consumer.

Section 810 Multiple Debts

If any consumer owes multiple debts and makes any single payment to any debt collector with respect to such debts, such debt collector may not apply such payment to any debt which is disputed by the consumer, and, where applicable, shall not apply such payment in accordance with the consumer's directions.

Section 811 Legal Actions by Debt Collectors

(a) Any debt collector who brings any legal action on a debt against any consumer shall —

(1) in case of any action to enforce an interest in real property securing the consumer's obligation, bring such action only in a judicial district or similar legal entity in which such real property is located; or

(2) in the case of an action not described in paragraph (1), bring such action only in a judicial district or similar length entity —

(A) in which such consumer signed the contract sued upon; or

(B) in which such consumer resides at the commencement of the action.

(b) Nothing in this title shall be construed to authorize the bringing of legal actions by debt collectors.

Section 812 Furnishing Certain Deceptive Forms

(a) It is unlawful to design, compile, and furnish any form knowing that such form would be used to create false belief in a consumer that a person other than the creditor of such consumer is participating in the collection of or in an attempt to collect a debt such consumer allegedly owes such creditor, when the fact is such person is not so participating.

(b) Any person who violated this section shall be liable to the same extent and in the same manner as a debt collector is liable under section 813 for failure to comply with a provision of this title.

APPENDIX D

*Debt Counseling
Services*

Credi-Care, Inc., of South Dakota
P.O. Box 3265
Rapid City, SD 57709-3269

Family Service Association of America
44 E. 23rd St.
New York, NY 10010

National Foundation for Consumer Credit, Inc.
8701 Georgia Ave.
Silver Springs, MD 20910

The Budget and Credit Counseling Service
115 E. 23rd St., 11th Floor
New York, NY 10010

APPENDIX E

Secured Credit Cards

First Consumers National Bank
Lincoln Center Tower
10260 Southwest Greenberg Road, Suite 600
Portland, OR 97223

Home Trust Savings and Loan
Card Center
P.O. Box 37
Brookings, SD 57006

Key Federal
153 Chestnut Hill Road
Newark, DE 19713

New Era Bank
P.O. Box 15414
Wilmington, DE 19713

Pioneer First Federal Savings and Loan
4111 200th St., S.W.
Lynwood, WA 98036

Service One International
21032 Devonshire, Suite 215
Chatsworth, CA 91311

Standard Savings and Loan
888 North Hill St.
Los Angeles, CA 90012

APPENDIX F

Credit Card Rating Services

Bankcard Holders of America
333 Pennsylvania, S.E., Dept. L
Washington, D.C. 20003

Bank Credit Card Observer
3086 Old Lincoln Highway, Suite 6
Kendall Park, NJ 08824-1658

Consumer Credit Card Rating Service
P.O. Box 5219
Ocean Park Station
Santa Monica, CA 90405

APPENDIX G

Loans by Mail

Bankers Investment Co.
Bankers Investment Building
Lock Drawer 334, P.O. Box 1648
Hutchinson, KS 67501

Citicorp Person-to-Person "Readicredit"
3033 South Parker Rd.
Aurora, CO 80014

Postal Executive Financial Services, Inc.
14201 E. Fourth Ave., P.O. Box 39
Denver, CO 80239

APPENDIX H

Addresses of Federal Agencies

THE VARIOUS FEDERAL CONSUMER CREDIT LAWS presented in this book are enforced by federal agencies. If you would like further information or have a particular credit problem that you would like answered, you can contact the appropriate agencies.

If your problem is with a retail department store, consumer finance company, all other creditors, all nonbank credit card issuers, credit bureaus, or debt collectors, write to:
    Division of Credit Practices
    Federal Trade Commission
    Washington, D.C. 20580

If you have a problem with a particular national bank, write to:
    Office of the Comptroller of the Currency
    Deputy Comptroller for Customer and Community
        Programs
    Department of the Treasury, 6th Floor
    L'Enfant Plaza
    Washington, D.C. 20219

If you have a problem with a particular state member bank, write to:
    Federal Reserve Board
    Division of Consumer and Community Affairs
    20th and C St.s, N.W.
    Washington, D.C. 20551

If you have a problem with a particular nonmember insured bank, or if you are uncertain of your bank's chartering (state or national), write to:
    Federal Deposit Insurance Corporation
    Office of Consumer Compliance Programs
    550 17th St., N.W.
    Washington, D.C. 20429

If you have a problem with a particular savings institution insured by the Federal Savings and Loan Insurance Corporation and member of the Federal Home Loan Bank System, write to:
    Federal Home Loan Bank Board
    Department of Consumer and Civil Rights
    Office of Examination and Supervision
    Washington, D.C. 20522

If you have a problem with a federal credit union write to:
    National Credit Union Administration
    Office of Consumer Affairs
    1776 G St., N.W.
    Washington, D.C. 20456

Many of these federal agencies have regional offices. Check your local telephone book under "United States Government" to see if there is a regional office near you.

APPENDIX I

Federal Trade Commission Offices

THE FEDERAL TRADE COMMISSION is the agency responsible for enforcing the Consumer Protection Act. If a company has violated your rights under any of these laws, you can file a complaint with the nearest regional office.

Headquarters
Pennsylvania Ave. and Sixth St., N.W.
Washington, D.C. 20580

Regional Offices
1718 Peachtree St., N.W.
Atlanta, GA 30367

10 Causeway St.
Boston, MA 02222

55 East Monroe St.
Chicago, IL 60603

8303 Elmbrook Dr.
Dallas, TX 75247

1405 Curtis St.
Denver, CO 80202

11000 Wilshire Blvd.
Los Angeles, CA 90024

26 Federal Plaza
New York, NY 10278

901 Market St.
San Francisco, CA 94103

915 Second Ave.
Seattle, WA 98174

APPENDIX J

State Banking Authorities

THE OFFICIALS LISTED BELOW regulate and supervise state-chartered banks. Many of them handle or refer problems and complaints concerning other types of financial institutions as well as answering general questions about banking and consumer credit.

Alabama
Mr. Zack Thompson
Superintendent of Banks
166 Commerce St., 3rd Floor
Montgomery, AL 36130

Alaska
Mr. Willis F. Kirkpatrick
Director of Banking and Securities
Pouch D
Juneau, AK 99811

Arizona
Ms. Mary C. Short
Superintendent of Banks
3225 North Central, Suite 815
Phoenix, AZ 85012

Arkansas
Mr. Marlin D. Jackson
Bank Commissioner
Tower Building
323 Center St., Suite 500
Little Rock, AR 72201

California
Mr. Howard Gould
Superintendent of Banks
235 Montgomery St., Suite 750
San Francisco, CA 94104

Colorado
Mr. Richard B. Doby
State Bank Commissioner
Colorado Division of Banking
First West Plaza, Suite 700
303 West Colfax
Denver, CO 80204

Connecticut
Mr. Howard B. Brown, Jr.
Banking Commissioner
44 Capitol Ave.
Hartford, CT 06106

Delaware
Mr. John E. Malarkey
State Bank Commissioner
P.O. Box 1401
Dover, DE 19903

District of Columbia
Mr. Edward D. Irons
Acting Superintendent of Banking
  and Financial Institutions
1350 Pennsylvania Ave., N W.
Room 401
Washington, DC 20004

Florida
Mr. Gerald Lewis
State Comptroller
State Capitol Building
Tallahassee, FL 32399

Georgia
Mr. Edward D. Dunn
Commissioner of Banking and Finance
2990 Brandywine Road, Suite 200
Atlanta, GA 30341

Guam
Mr. Dave J. Santos
Banking Commissioner
P.O. Box 2796
Agana, GU 96910
(Written inquiries only)

Hawaii
Ms. Donna Tanoue
Bank Examiner
P.O. Box 541
Honolulu, HI 96809

Idaho
Mr. Belton J. Patty
Director Department of Finance
700 West State St., 2nd Floor
Boise, ID 83720

Illinois
Mr. William C. Harris
Commissioner of Banks and Trust Companies
119 South Fifth St., Room 400
Springfield, IL 62701

Indiana
Ms. Ruth D. Harrison
Director Department of Financial Institutions
Indiana State Office Building, Room 1024
Indianapolis, IN 46204

Iowa
Mr. William R. Bernau
Superintendent of Banking
200 East Grand, Suite 300
Des Moines, IA 50309

Kansas
Mr. Eugene T. Barrett, Jr.
State Bank Commissioner
700 Jackson St., Suite 300
Topeka, KS 66603

Kentucky
Mr. Thomas B. Miller
Commissioner of Banking and Securities
911 Leawood Drive
Frankfort, KY 40601

Louisiana
Mr. Fred C. Dent, Jr.
Commissioner of Financial Institutions
P.O. Box 94095
Baton Rouge, LA 70804

Maine
Mr. H. Donald DeMatteis
Superintendent of Banking
State House Station #36
Augusta, ME 04333

Maryland
Ms. Margie H. Muller
Bank Commissioner
34 Market Place
Baltimore, MD 21202

Massachusetts
Mr. Paul E. Bulman
Commissioner of Banks
100 Cambridge St.
Boston, MA 02202

Michigan
Mr. Eugene W. Kuthy
Commissioner Financial Institutions Bureau
P.O. Box 30224
Lansing, MI 48909

Minnesota
Mr. James G. Miller
Deputy Commissioner of Commerce
500 Metro Square Building, 5th Floor
St. Paul, MN 55101

Mississippi
Ms. Jean S. Porter, Commissioner
Department of Banking and Consumer Finance
P.O. Box 731
Jackson, MS 39205

Missouri
Mr. Thomas B. Fitzsimmons
Commissioner of Finance
P.O. Box 716
Jefferson City, MO 65102

Montana
Mr. Fred J. Flanders
Commissioner of Financial Institutions
1424 Ninth Ave.
Helena, MT 59620

Nebraska
Ms. Cynthia H. Milligan
Director of Banking and Finance
301 Centennial Mall, South
Lincoln, NE 68509

Nevada
Mr. L. Scott Walshaw
Commissioner of
Financial Institutions
406 East Second St.
Carson City, NV 89710

New Hampshire
Mr. A. Roland Roberge
Bank Commissioner
45 South Main St.
Concord, NH 03301

New Jersey
Ms. Mary Little Parell
Commissioner of Banking
36 West State St.
Trenton, NJ 08625

New Mexico
Mr. James W. Stretz, Director
Financial Institutions Division
Bataan Memorial Bldg., Room 137
Santa Fe, NM 87503

New York
Ms. Jill M. Considine
Superintendent of Banks
Two Rector St.
New York, NY 10006

North Carolina
Mr. William T. Graham
Commissioner of Banks
P.O. Box 29512
Raleigh, NC 27626

North Dakota
Mr. Gary D. Preszler
Commissioner of Banking and Financial Institutions
State Capitol, Room 1301
Bismarck, ND 58505

Ohio
Ms. Linda K. Page
Superintendent of Banks
Two Nationwide Plaza
Columbus, OH 43215

Oklahoma
Mr. Robert Y. Empie
Bank Commissioner
Malco Bldg.
4100 North Lincoln Blvd.
Oklahoma City, OK 73105

Oregon
Mr. Cecil R. Monroe
Deputy Administrator
Financial Institutions Division
260 Court St., N.E.
Salem, OR 97310

Pennsylvania
Ms. Sarah W. Hargrove
Secretary of Banking
333 Market St., 16th Floor
Harrisburg, PA 17101

Puerto Rico
Ms. Angel L. Rosas
Commissioner of Banking
P.O. Box S4515
San Juan, PR 00905

Rhode Island
Ms. Susan D. Hayes
Assistant Director
Banking and Securities
100 North Main St.
Providence, RI 02903

South Carolina
Mr. Robert C. Cleveland
Commissioner of Banking
1026 Sumter St., Room 217
Columbia, SC 29201

South Dakota
Mr. Richard A. Duncan
Director of Banking and Finance
State Capitol Bldg.
Pierre, SD 57501

Tennessee
Mr. Dennis R. Phillips
Commissioner of Financial Institutions
John Sevier Bldg., 4th Floor
Nashville, TN 37219

Texas
Mr. Kenneth W. Littlefield
Banking Commissioner
2601 North Lamar
Austin, TX 78705

Utah
Mr. George Sutton
Commissioner of Financial Insitutions
P.O. Box 89
Salt Lake City, UT 84110

Vermont
Mr. Thomas P. Menson
Commissioner of Banking and Insurance
State Office Bldg.
Montpelier, VT 05602

Virgin Islands
Mr. Julio A. Brady
Lieutenant Governor
Chairman of the Banking Board
Kongens Gardens #18
P.O. Box 450
St. Thomas, VI 00801

Virginia
Mr. Sidney A. Bailey
Commissioner of Financial Institutions
P.O. Box 2-AE
Richmond, VA 23205

Washington
Mr. Thomas H. Oldfield
Supervisor of Banking
General Administration Bldg., Room 219
Olympia, WA 98504

West Virginia
Mr. David F. Mudie
Deputy Commissioner of Banking
State Office Bldg. 3, Suite 311
Charleston, WV 25305

Wisconsin
Mr. Richard E. Galecki
Commissioner of Banking
P.O. Box 7876
Madison, WI 53707

Wyoming
Mr. Stanley R. Hunt
State Examiner
Herschler Bldg., 4th Floor
Cheyenne, WY 82002

Rules for Safe Credit Card Use

1. Keep a list of your credit card numbers, expiration dates, and the number of each card issuer in a secure place.
2. Credit card issuers offer a wide variety of terms (annual percentage rate, methods of calculating the balance subject to the finance charge, minimum monthly payments, and actual membership fees). When selecting a card, compare the terms offered by several card issuers to find the one that best suits your needs.
3. Watch your card after giving it to a clerk. Take your card back promptly after the clerk is finished with it and make sure it's yours.
4. Tear up the carbons when you take your credit card receipt. Void or destroy any incorrect receipts.
5. Never sign a blank receipt. Draw a line through any blank spaces above the total when you sign receipts.
6. Open credit card bills promptly and compare them with your receipts to check for unauthorized charges and billing errors.

7. Report promptly and in writing to the card issuer any questionable charges. Written inquiries should not be included with your payment. Check the billing statement for the correct address to send any written inquiries. The inquiry must be in writing to guarantee your rights.

8. Never give out your credit card number over the telephone unless you have initiated the call.

9. Never put your card number on a postcard or on the outside of an envelope.

10. Sign new cards as soon as they arrive. Cut up expired cards and dispose of them promptly. Cut up and return unwanted cards to the issuer.

11. Leave infrequently used cards in a secure place.

12. If any of your credit cards are missing or stolen, report them as soon as possible to your card issuers. Some companies have 24-hour service and toll-free numbers printed on their statements for this purpose. For your own protection, follow up your phone calls with a letter to each issuer. The letter should contain your card number, the date the card was missing, and the date you called in the loss.

13. If you report the loss before a credit card is used, the issuer cannot hold you responsible for any subsequent unauthorized charges. If a thief uses your card before you report it missing, the most you will owe for unauthorized charges on each card is $50.

APPENDIX K

Resources

PUBLICATIONS

Credit Secrets: How to Erase Bad Credit
Bob Hammond
Paladin Press
P.O. Box 1307
Boulder, CO 80306

Contains a detailed description of the identification systems used by each of the major credit bureaus, along with dynamic strategies for circumventing the system and starting over with a new credit file. Also describes a unique method of "losing" your bankruptcy files and deleting any reference to filing for Chapter 7 or Chapter 13.

How to Beat the Credit Bureaus: The Insider's Guide to Consumer Credit
Bob Hammond
Paladin Press

In this intriguing follow-up to his best-selling first book, *Credit Secrets*, author Bob Hammond describes the deceptive web of information systems spun by the powerful corporate credit bureau syndicate and how it is used to victim-ize, humiliate, and defile countless innocent consumers. More importantly, it will show you how to take legal action against an unfair system—and win. Includes documented successful lawsuits against major credit-reporting agencies. This book is must reading for every American consumer.

ABOUT THE AUTHOR

BOB HAMMOND IS THE AUTHOR of *Credit Secrets: How to Erase Bad Credit* and *How to Beat the Credit Bureaus: The Insider's Guide to Consumer Credit* (both available from Paladin Press).

Hammond is also the editor of the *Directory of Consumer Credit Services* (Consumer Research) and has provided credit consulting to countless individuals, business organizations, civic groups, and governmental agencies. He is a member of the Consumer Credit Commission, which is a consumer-rights organization, and the Author's Guild.

Highly sought after as a consumer advocate, Hammond conducts radio interviews, as well as lectures and seminars, on the issues facing a cashless society.

RELATED READING

How to File for Bankruptcy (Nolo, 1990) by attorneys Elias, Renaur, and Leonard is a practical guide for this approach, as a do-it-yourself kit for Chapter 7 bankruptcy. Most consumers, however, require more than just a band-aid solution to their problems.

How to Get Out of Debt, Stay Out of Debt, and Live Prosperously (New York: Bantam, 1988) by Jerrold Mundis tells readers that bankruptcy is not even an option. This extreme view limits a person's available alternatives to spending plans and support groups. Based on the twelve-step program Debtor's Anonymous, it encourages people to give up credit spending altogether. This book falls short of dealing with the reality of the coming cashless society and does not address the practical needs of most consumers.

How to Improve Your Credit (EFG, 1988) by Richard Streb and *The Credit Power Handbook for American Consumers* (Credit Power, 1988) by Daniel Berman are among several credit-repair manuals that retail for $49.95. Others, like Michael Hsul's *How to Erase Bad Credit Successfully* (Business Credit Systems, 1988), sell for as much as $295. In spite of their popularity, these books offer little help to most consumers. They concentrate on out-dated methods, which are ineffective in most situations.

Books like *Financial Self-Defense* (New York: Simon and Shuster, 1990) by Charles Givens are aimed toward high-income investors and business executives. They fail to realize that most people are not in that category.

Out of Debt: Avoiding Bankruptcy (Bob Adams, 1989) by Robert Steinback also falls short of addressing the needs of people who lack income. Nor does it give much advice on establishing credit after a person has already filed for bankruptcy.

INDEX